STACEY A. GORDON

ADDRESSING

UNCONSCIOUS

BIAS AT WORK

WILEY

Published by John Wiley & Sons, Inc., Hoboken, New Jersey.
Published simultaneously in Canada.

For general information on our other products and services or for technical support, please contact our Customer Care Department within the United States at (800) 762-2974, outside the United States at (317) 572-3993 or fax (317) 572-4002.

Wiley publishes in a variety of print and electronic formats and by print-on-demand. Some material included with standard print versions of this book may not be included in e-books or in print-on-demand. If this book refers to media such as a CD or DVD that is not included in the version you purchased, you may download this material at http://booksupport.wiley.com. For more information about Wiley products, visit www.wiley.com.

Library of Congress Cataloging-in-Publication Data:

Names: Gordon, Stacey A., author.
Title: Unbias : addressing unconscious bias at work / Stacey Gordon.
Description: Hoboken, New Jersey : Wiley, [2021] | Includes bibliographical
  references and index.
Identifiers: LCCN 2021003282 (print) | LCCN 2021003283 (ebook) | ISBN
  9781119779049 (hardback) | ISBN 9781119779063 (adobe pdf) | ISBN
  9781119779070 (epub)
Subjects: LCSH: Discrimination. | Subconsciousness. | Diversity in the
  workplace.
Classification: LCC HM821 .G6735 2021 (print) | LCC HM821 (ebook) | DDC
  331.13/3—dc23
LC record available at https://lccn.loc.gov/2021003282
LC ebook record available at https://lccn.loc.gov/2021003283

Cover Design: Wiley
Cover Image: © Shanina/Getty Images
SKY10025033_021721

Dedication

This book is dedicated to all the people who have worked tirelessly to improve workplaces for all without the recognition of a formal title, without the benefit of resources, and with nothing but the knowledge and desire that things need to change.

Contents

Introduction

Diversity, inclusion, bias – these can be sensitive topics that are difficult to talk about, especially at work. We are at a time when we don't know how to talk about sensitive topics. We've been taught to avoid them and now they are staring us in the face. I am writing this book in an election year when opinions about everything, including politics, have become extremely divided. Individuals are at opposing ends of the spectrum with no tools for how to listen to the point of view of another without name calling and labeling. We have been taught for so long not to discuss sex, politics, or religion, when what we should have been taught was how to constructively discuss sex, politics, and religion. And what is noticeably missing from what I call the three taboo terms is race. It is so ingrained in us not to discuss race that we don't even talk about the fact that we don't talk about race. It is no surprise then, that it is difficult for us to have conversations around race, gender, privilege, and other dimensions of diversity in the workplace.

It is also not surprising there is a reluctance and a lack of understanding around why we're having these conversations at work at all. I hear that work isn't the place for these conversations. We just come to work and do our jobs and that is what we should focus on.

These are excuses, and I will tackle those and many more throughout the book, but what I want to address is the chasm that is growing between individuals of different races. Why does it always have to be about race? Your *perception* may be that it is always about race, but it isn't. Unconscious bias at work, in your workplace, is about race, gender, sexual orientation, age, ability, religion, veteran status, socioeconomic background, education, culture, and geography.

We do keep coming back to race because we haven't addressed the issues of race and racism in the United States. The only way to get past race is to go through it. Winston Churchill said, "If you're going through hell, keep going," and we haven't kept going. We keep stopping because the road is tough, the conversations are uncomfortable, and the realization that what we've been doing for many years may have been wrong is difficult to face.

Fortunately for you, I have no qualms about diving in head-first and tackling the tough topics we need to address, and I'll do it by helping you to address unconscious bias at work.

1

The Blueprint

The number one question I am always asked when it comes to diversity and inclusion initiatives is "How will we know we're doing the right thing?" I have been asked several versions of this question in podcasts, at conferences, on panels, by CEOs, during a fireside chat, and in educational workshops by employees.

No one wants to get this wrong. Or at least, from what I have seen, no one wants to appear as if they don't care. However, the difference between whether you actually care or whether you care more about the appearance of seeming to care makes all the difference to your success.

The first question I ask company leaders when I am tasked with advising them on their next steps is "What is your strategy?" Unfortunately, it is no longer surprising that they answer all too frequently, "We don't know."

My goal is to answer both "How do we do this right?" and "What is your strategy?" because the answers to both of these questions are related.

The concept of diversity is difficult because there isn't a one-size-fits-all solution. What works for one company will not work for another. Companies like Ben & Jerry's are being applauded for their statements, their social media presence, and their loyal customer following, and business leaders want to be *that* company, but aren't willing to do the work it takes to get there. Instead, there is a belief that diversity is minimal, and inclusion is elusive. Business leaders make excuses and use them as a shield to absolve them of their duty as leaders to do the work.

Ben & Jerry's Exceeds the Bar

On April 18, 2016, the cofounders of Ben & Jerry's were arrested on the steps of the U.S. Capitol Building as part of a group of activists who were fighting for a better democracy. Right before they were arrested, Ben is quoted as saying, "The history of our country is that nothing happens until people start putting their bodies on the line and risk getting arrested."

In an interview with CNBC in June 2020, CEO Matthew McCarthy said, "Business should be held accountable to setting very specific targets, specifically around dismantling white supremacy in and through our organizations." He also said, "In businesses, in a lot of ways, you treasure what you measure. You measure what you treasure. If you don't put goals around these things, they simply don't happen."

Ben & Jerry's operates on a three-part mission that aims to create linked prosperity for everyone connected to their business: suppliers, employees, farmers, franchisees, customers, and neighbors alike. They have an economic mission to manage their company for sustainable financial growth, a social mission to use their company in innovative ways to make the world a better place, and a product mission to make fantastic ice cream. They are clear in those missions and ensure everyone else is too.

Their FAQ page answers questions like "What is Criminal Justice Reform?" and "Why would reforming cash bail be a good thing?" They post articles on their website that help people find their polling place, advocate for women's equality, and discuss racism in America.

Neither Ben nor Jerry have been shy about taking a stand and they are well known for creating ice cream flavors with big chunks, swirls, and textures that resonate around the world.

Some of those excuses include:

Diversity doesn't work.
I don't see color.
We just hire the best without regard to gender or race.
We don't want to lower the bar on job requirements.

I find these statements to be troublesome. At best they are ignorant, and at worst they build barriers to diversity by creating a culture where the status quo is acceptable. These statements create roadblocks to innovation by stifling the ability of leaders to harness the creativity of their workforce by restricting diversity.

These excuses stem from failing to be clear on your strategy. What is your motivation for wanting to take action? Do you have an authentic desire to change or is this a publicity stunt to placate your employees, customers, and investors?

The excuses also stem from failing to define organization values and align strategic diversity outcomes to those values. Do you know what you stand for as an organization? Do your employees know? Are you clear on which behaviors you will not tolerate in the workplace? Without a clear understanding of your organization's core values, it's impossible to embed effective diversity strategies into your systems and processes. Chapter 3 further discusses the establishment of values and how that relates to real organizational change.

Failure to create accountability in your senior leadership team is yet another area that cultivates these excuses. Do your leaders have clarity on what is expected of them and what their role is in creating an inclusive workplace? Do they know what level of ownership they have?

Have resources been allocated? Commitment goes beyond words. We focus on the failure to allocate time, energy, and dollars, but the failure to allocate decision-making power is often overlooked. Without the ability to hold others accountable, your policies and procedures have no teeth.

Doing "the right thing" is difficult when you don't have information to direct your actions. The excuses that leaders rely on also stem from a failure to obtain data and create achievable metrics. How do you know if the needle moved when you don't know where it was when you began?

The Framework of the Blueprint

I work to remove barriers and reduce bias as a mission, but my mission is only successful when yours is too. The blueprint I work from is my own strategy that, when applied across the commonalities of business, provides a place from which to measure how close you are to achieving your goal. In my experience working with thousands of employees at companies around the globe, I have encountered common themes, common challenges, and common solutions that run across industries, across company sizes, and across cultures.

The basic framework is the same for each organization, whether you have one hundred employees or one hundred thousand. Where the difference lies is in the implementation. With the opportunity to observe actions and behaviors, as well as to begin to recognize the mindsets that drive them, I have been able to classify companies into four main levels or phases: Awareness, Alignment, Action, and Advocacy.

The categories collectively characterize the practices, policies, and procedures that an organization needs to address and the order in which to do it. While the concepts around diversity and inclusion may come from a U.S.-centric lens, they are applicable globally. I also use the term "inclusive workplace" to refer to the concept that company leaders must create a culture that is accepting of individual differences. However, when you consider the vast number of dimensions of diversity in the Four Layers model (see Figure 1.1), you can see they influence each other, which is why intersectionality is so important (but I'm getting ahead of myself). That convergence and influence of dimensions is what can make this work seem difficult, and as you'll hear me say repeatedly, "Complex doesn't have to mean difficult and it definitely isn't impossible."

You've probably also heard it said that you cannot have inclusion without diversity, but you cannot have an inclusive workplace culture without an organization that respects the diversity of the individuals, acknowledges the value that diversity brings to the organization, and actively works to ensure all employees within the organization are included in the practices, policies, and procedures of the workplace.

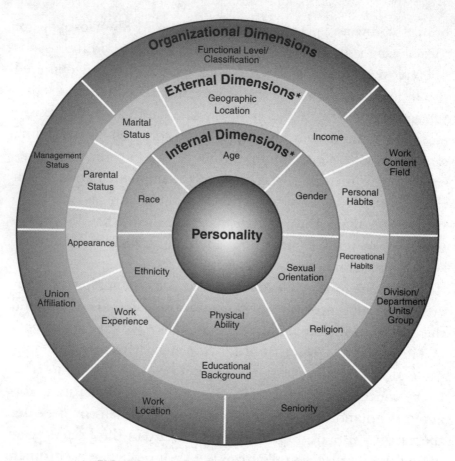

FIGURE 1.1 The Four Layers of Diversity.

Sources: Lee Gardenswartz and Anita Rowe, *Diverse Teams at Work*, 2nd Edition (Society for Human Resource Management, 2003); Adapted from Marilyun Loden and Judy Rosener, *Workforce America* (Business One Irwin, 1991).

Awareness

The Awareness phase is the starting point for any organization's journey into diversity, equity, and inclusion. The goal is to become aware of the current state of your organization. It sounds much simpler than it is because this phase informs your strategy. It provides guidance and direction by surfacing the challenges to increasing diversity and creating inclusion while simultaneously offering evidence of what is working and what you should do more of.

Obtaining the data and the artifacts that will drive your pursuit of greater awareness can be done through several means. Surveys, focus groups, townhall meetings, feedback/suggestion boxes, and interviews can be used independently or in concert with one another to create a robust vehicle for listening to your employees.

This phase is not all about data and metrics. In each phase, there is an overarching need for education and communication. When working to "wake up" your organization leaders and employees as a whole, transparency of decisions being made is just as important as requesting feedback, while foundational diversity, equity, and inclusion concepts help stakeholders begin to see how their participation, or lack thereof, impacts the overall strategy.

As a way of illustration, let's take a look at Lisa, a figurative CEO of a made-up tech company with 100 employees. Lisa and her counterparts in other departments have been given direction by their superiors to look into how diverse and inclusive their departments are. Lisa's first instinct is to reach out to Human Resources (HR) to get the demographic breakdown of her staff, assuming that boosting the number of underrepresented minorities should suffice to appease all parties. However, after a few minutes on the phone with the HR manager, she discovers that a handful of complaints regarding a hostile work environment have been filed anonymously and never addressed. Lisa realizes that she's going to have to dig a lot deeper to truly get a picture of how her department is doing and how to approach the damage that's already been done.

To completely move through the phases and reach Advocacy, this initial phase of Awareness makes it clear that diversity and inclusion within organizations does not only begin by increasing the number of represented identities across gender, race, ethnicity, ability, and age. An organization must undergo a process to become diverse and inclusive, one that starts with assessing how they are practicing the key elements in those core concepts. These elements are found in the experiences of your employees and it is imperative they are captured through metrics, data, and other investigative tools, which I will discuss in greater detail in Chapter 6.

Learning the state of your workplace culture provides you with a starting point to begin to answer the question of "How do we do this right?" Assessment of trust, communication, and other key elements that are the roots of diversity and inclusion will provide you and your organization with a place your leadership team can begin to align on future action.

Alignment

In the Alignment phase, your organization leaders will utilize the information provided in the Awareness phase, which provided clarity around the current state of the organization and start to align on the strategy. Determining the direction and agreeing to support the strategy is an important and fundamental factor.

In this phase, education is again present to reinforce the knowledge that diversity and inclusion within organizations does not only begin by increasing the number of represented identities across gender, race, ethnicity, ability, and age. It is understood that an organization must undergo a process to become diverse and inclusive, and it continues by assessing how key elements in those core concepts are being practiced. To do so, there must be a shared understanding of what diversity and inclusion is rooted in and how it is important for the organization.

After months of one-on-one interviews and focus groups, Lisa's HR team has gathered eye-opening, experiential data from her employees about the state of the organization. As she discusses her discoveries and proposed path forward with department managers, she learns that several of them felt the "diversity" assignment wasn't really a priority, that what mattered most was the optics of looking like they made an effort while still increasing the company's overall revenue. Lisa leaves the meeting frustrated and disappointed by the company's disjointed viewpoint.

The pillars of diversity and inclusion are held in the beliefs, actions, and practices of an organization, from employee to leadership. The objective of the Alignment phase is to educate everyone on the critical components of a diverse, equitable, and inclusive workplace in order to practice and thus cultivate this in the organization. It is incumbent upon the leadership to authentically embrace this knowledge. To get the leadership team to buy in and commit to diversity and inclusion, the leaders have to align on the direction as well as the value to the company. Lisa and her team have a lot of meetings in their future because without alignment on the need to reach the goal, they have no hope of aligning on a strategy to achieve it. They have to help the leadership team see how unconscious bias is affecting each and every department and receive commitments to do something about it.

One additional outcome of the Alignment phase is the setting of expectations. This phase creates accountability in leadership and demands action as a next step. Demonstrating support for the strategy provides clarity, as well as trust, to the workforce and sets the expectation that action will follow. Failing to move to the Action phase destroys the momentum that has been built, casts doubt on the data that has been obtained, and erodes trust in your leadership team.

Action

This phase is where everyone thinks they want to start because of its label. "Action" is what everyone wants to do, but what they actually mean by "action" is really only offering unconscious bias education. (See the next chapter for what I think about that.) This phase requires actual action. This is where you do the work of reviewing and revising the practices, policies, and procedures of your organization and to do that, accountability, transparency, and authenticity will be required if the end result you seek is a truly inclusive workplace.

With her company's leadership finally aligned on its values and the import of a diverse and inclusive workplace, Lisa is now ready to start rocking the boat in her department. She begins by engaging the head of every department, from sales to research and development to marketing, to discuss ways to remove the barriers to true inclusion in their work environment.

Action means working to identify the places where bias and inequities continue to lurk. Upon discussion, there must be a deeper practice of inclusive leadership – role-modeling the action that will be required to be taken to do the work.

Action means dismantling the practice of only hiring individuals from Ivy League colleges. Action means reviewing compensation across your organization and paying women and men the same salary for the same job. Action means working with the architect to ensure the new office you're building will not just be ADA compliant, but accessible. Action is determining why 30% of your workforce is diverse yet every leadership role is filled by a white man. Action is understanding why, on average, women leave your company after five years; it means pinpointing the challenge and then actually fixing the issue.

Advocacy

Reaching the Advocacy phase is something not very many organizations achieve. Not because of the difficulty, but because of the prior stages. So many companies try to begin with the Action phase when they are actually in the Awareness phase. However, without knowing that, they apply task-oriented thinking to what should be strategic planning, resulting in an initiative that is short-lived, under-resourced, and without direction.

Lisa's department managers have finally bought into the value of a diverse and inclusive workplace as a result of upper management's valuation of its concepts. In turn, employees at all levels have begun to embrace the newly revised policies and procedures that address the unconscious bias we all harbor, remove the barriers the systems have created, and weave diversity and inclusion initiatives into the very foundation of the company and its mission. While she knows that her company, and the people in it, can never be completely bias-free, she is optimistic that the conversations will continue in a way that allows issues to be identified and addressed with more expediency.

In the phase of Advocacy, not only do you have current-state knowledge of your organization, with an understanding of where your organization is as it relates to foundational DEI (diversity, equity, and inclusion) concepts and metrics, but also you have grasped the "why" of moving forward along the path to becoming an inclusive organization. Your organization leaders understand, support, and have aligned on the strategy. They fully support the concept that diversity and inclusion within organizations is not only focused on the traditional notions of diversity. They have consistently reviewed and revised their practices, policies, and procedures and are role-modeling accountability, transparency, and authenticity. In the phase of advocacy, the cultivation of an inclusive workplace is reached when every person in the organization is working together to make sustainability of diversity and inclusion a priority.

There is no single "right thing" or "right way" to support diversity and create a culture of inclusion in the workplace. This framework provides a guide, and throughout this book the various methods and recommended activities can be implemented in numerous configurations. Don't get hung up on the definitions or the structure; instead focus on your strategy and successful attainment of your goal.

PART

1

Awareness

2

Start with Unconscious Bias?

So, you want to offer unconscious bias training for your organization? You are not alone. Like you and your company, the world collectively woke up on May 25, 2020, with the tragic murder of George Floyd. Or maybe it took your company a little bit longer to get to the realization there is a deep disconnect in society and it has been negatively impacting your workplace for many years.

Prior to May 25, 2020, it was a little easier to ignore the calls for social justice. It was easier to believe that "this is a workplace, and we don't need to address that here." Or you may have been one of the company leaders who was working on change before May 2020 but were spurred along to act more quickly, whether you liked it or not.

While May 25, 2020, may have been a lightning strike, the dry brush was already smoldering. There was a demand for marriage equality, a push to destigmatize hiring recently incarcerated individuals, and we watched the privileged cheat their way into college, alongside the realization that attending a high-ranked university doesn't equate to career success. The amalgamation of these realities, in addition to the Black Lives Matter movement, started a fire companies can no longer ignore.

George Floyd Sparked a Global Outcry

On May 25, 2020, George Floyd, an unarmed Black man, died after a white police officer, in an attempt to arrest him, knelt on his neck for nearly nine minutes as he lay on a sidewalk in Minneapolis, Minnesota.

His death sparked global protests that were captured in more than 77 countries, including the UK, Hong Kong, New Zealand, Kenya, Brazil, China, Japan, and India. The protests began in Minneapolis, where the four officers present during his murder were fired. While protests continued for many weeks and were documented in cities across every state within the U.S., the question remains, "Why did this particular death cause such an outcry?"

He was not the first Black man in police custody – and unfortunately he probably won't be the last – to say, "I can't breathe," before being pronounced dead.

On July 17, 2014, Eric Garner died in Staten Island, a borough of New York City, after a New York City police department officer put him in a prohibited chokehold while attempting to arrest him. In the video footage that captured his death, Garner can be heard repeatedly stating that he can't breathe.

The application to the workplace comes in the understanding that there are injustices in the world and a good leader realizes they cannot be blind to the fact that injustices in the world will equate to injustices in the workplace.

No one leaves bias and bigotry at the door when they come to work, so while you cannot change people's beliefs, you can change their behavior in the workplace.

This book is a resource to guide you through the steps for leading your company through unprecedented change and to tackle various types of unconscious bias along the way. The information in this book is the culmination of more than a decade of my professional experience working with clients in the capacity of recruiter, coach, and diversity consultant as well as the more than four decades of personal experience navigating the world as a Black woman. So one of the first biases we will tackle is what you might think about me.

Making Assumptions

You may have made assumptions about what I believe, who I am, where I'm from, and how those things might affect the information you're about to get. But bias isn't only about race and no matter where in the world you are, there are hundreds of ways we can be biased. However, race always enters the discussion because it's easiest to spot.

But consider this. I am black and I am female, two things you can usually tell just by looking at me. What you can't possibly know just by looking at me is whether I'm heterosexual, where I was born, my status as a citizen in the United States, if I have children, how old I am, where I live, how much money I have in the bank, who I pray to or whether I pray at all, who I voted for in the past presidential election, or whether I have a college degree.

So I'd like you to take a moment to ask yourself what you actually know about me. And if that is nothing, I'll ask you not to put words in my mouth before I've had the chance to say them.

More than 150,000 individuals have gone through my course on unconscious bias on LinkedIn Learning in English. It has also been translated into Mandarin, Portuguese, Spanish, and Japanese and the number one comment I receive can be boiled down to "It was surprisingly informative." I make an assumption that the course was "surprisingly informative" because viewers took the course with the expectation that it would not in fact be informative at all. I may even go so far as to say that many may have believed it would push an agenda that was different from theirs and they were ready to hate it. I say that because I have also received those comments from quite a few individuals who were mandated to take the course and they have blatantly said as much. Comments included:

> *I just finished taking your unconscious bias course through my company and it was better than I thought it would be. Great job on delivery.*

> *Thank you for putting together a training on bias that was actually unbiased.*

> *I really enjoyed your course on "Unconscious Bias". . . it has made me pause and think and hopefully change my actions going forward . . . It was unexpectedly insightful!!*

All that is to say, if you're at all skeptical about my motives for this book, I'd like you to know I understand why you might feel that way, and I'm still going to ask that you save your assumptions until the end.

Unconscious Bias: Diversity and Incusion as a Strategy

With that being said, I will return to your need for unconscious bias education. Unconscious bias as a topic is seen as a solution to tackling the diversity and inclusion issues that companies now find themselves faced with. Companies have become global organizations, whether they intend to or not, and these organizations can't operate without people. While that may seem obvious, people are a network of teams; they thrive on engagement, need open dialogue, and are an amalgamation of inclusive working styles. Diversity and inclusion need to be a comprehensive strategy embedded into each and every aspect of the talent life cycle.

CEOs are beginning to take ownership of this strategy and this is revealed in a 2017 Global Human Capital Trends report by Deloitte. According to that report, 69% of executives see diversity and inclusion as important. And this is an increase from their 2014 survey, where only 59% of executives saw it as important. In 2020, belonging, along with well-being, is at the top of the Global Human Capital Trends survey as one of the most important human capital issues; 79% of survey respondents said that fostering a sense of belonging in the workforce was important to their organization's success in the next 12–18 months, and 93% agreed that a sense of belonging drives organizational performance – one of the highest rates of consensus on importance they have seen in a decade of Global Human Capital Trends reports.[1]

The Need to Ask "Why?"

Why should your organization prioritize diversity and inclusion now? Why should unconscious bias education be a priority? These are questions that you will have to answer, and it will be difficult to do so. "Why" puts people on the defensive. "Why" makes people uncomfortable. "Why" requires an explanation, which then requires you to dig deep for an answer. When it comes to unconscious bias at work, there's the possibility that you won't like what you find when you start digging.

However, "why" is the very thing you need to know when embarking on a journey to tackle unconscious bias and create an inclusive workplace. Just ask leadership expert Simon Sinek. In his book *Start with Why: How Great Leaders Inspire Everyone to Take Action*, he explains that answering the why can inspire cooperation, trust, and change. Why does unconscious bias education matter to you? The only way to answer that question is to understand what matters to your company. What is the goal and mission of your business? You may discover that diversity, inclusion, belonging, and creating a great workplace culture don't actually matter to your company at all, depending upon what you value. If you're unsure about your company's core values, you'll find further detail about this in the next chapter, but for now it's enough to understand that the motivation behind your decision to prioritize diversity and inclusion should stem from your organization's foundational values.

---

[1] https://www2.deloitte.com/content/dam/insights/us/articles/us43244_human-capital-trends-2020/us43244_human-capital-trends-2020/di_hc-trends-2020.pdf.

The Bandwagon Effect

When I worked at Prudential many years ago, there were teams of advisors whose job was to identify individuals who needed a financial advisor, convince them they were the right advisor for them, and then sell them a product. If you've ever worked in sales, you probably recognize these directives. Our teams were created by our manager, and living in Los Angeles, California, you might assume those teams were very diverse. And you would be very wrong.

The job of the advisor is to convince the client they are the best advisor for them. It is the basic tenant of any sales job. When selling, you are told to mirror potential clients, find things in common, get them to like you. There are thousands of sales education materials on the market showing salespeople how to sell. This is called the bandwagon effect, but did you know it's actually an unconscious bias? The bandwagon effect harnesses our need to want what everyone else wants. In sales, that's great. If you can show that you're the top realtor, the best advisor, or the most sought-after designer, you have a much higher likelihood of closing the potential client. It's also why sales professionals love referrals. If they were referred to you by a current client, the odds of closing the deal increases dramatically. But that's the trouble with all of this. We connect with people in our circle, we refer people in our circle, and our circles aren't usually very diverse.

If you were to look at a demographic survey for our Prudential office, it would not demonstrate diversity. At least, not if you analyzed the data carefully. Our teams of advisors ended up being highly segregated. If you were Chinese, you were recruited by the Chinese manager and you were hired to a team that was 80% Chinese. Of course if you were not Chinese and you happened to make it onto that team, you did not last very long because you did not speak Mandarin or Cantonese, you did not understand the culture, you were not invited to attend client meetings if the client was Chinese, and not only did you *feel* excluded, you *were* excluded. You didn't perform as well as the other members on your team and in a commission-only sales environment, you eventually quit.

This didn't only happen with the Chinese managers. It happened with the Korean managers, the Armenian managers, and the white managers. It also happened with female managers. A demographic survey of the office where I worked would be beautifully diverse on the surface. It would show that we had a vast array of individuals who were ethnically and racially diverse, spoke a number of languages, and even had decent gender diversity. But you would have to take a further look at the data to really see that the diversity was actually segmented, not through policy, but through human behavior and our desire for affinity.

Prudential was by no means an anomaly. One of my coaching clients worked for an investment management company for almost three years. The accounts were a minimum size of $2 million and he did a great job managing the money under his care. He made sound investments and increased portfolio size tremendously. He should have been on a trajectory to lead a client account, but instead he quit his very lucrative job after being told by his white manager that their high-net-worth clients wouldn't be comfortable with him, a Black man, being their account manager. Without the opportunity to become a fund manager, he would be unable to lead a team and essentially had no opportunity for advancement.

Unconscious Bias Is a Complex Issue: Defining Your Why

One of the reasons addressing diversity, inclusion, and unconscious bias at work can seem difficult is that it is usually a complex problem. You don't normally have one straightforward issue to be resolved. There is nuance and it is multifaceted, which makes you have to work a little harder to unravel it all. It is necessary to tackle both the lack of diversity and the lack of "why," and the process can be complex. However, complex does not automatically equate to difficult.

When a company is unable to discern why diversity and inclusion training is a priority for them, the default answer is often "to avoid bad publicity." If we look at the Black Lives Matter movement as an example, your company might be one of the many who published a statement of support for George Floyd and told everyone that "Black Lives Matter" in an attempt to avoid being put on the list of companies to boycott. Maintaining good optics is not a "why." It is inauthentic, not actionable, and your consumers, clients, and employees see right through it.

Numerous statistics indicate the positive financial impact of diversity and inclusion on the workplace. Companies that are inclusive are more likely to lead and capture new markets, 43% of companies with diverse management exhibited higher profits, companies with racial and ethnical diversity are 35% more likely to perform at a higher level, and companies with an equal number of men and women produce up to 41% higher revenues.

It's no wonder that in the absence of a why, the default answer is "to make money," and we assume because we need to make money and our clients won't work with someone who doesn't look like them, that there is nothing that can be done about the lack of diversity. We throw up our hands and say that it is what it is. Yet when you have a true "why," making money becomes a happy by-product. A company that truly understands this concept is Vans, the footwear company. When a call was made to support Black-owned businesses, they made it difficult to purchase anything on their website that day. On July 7, 2020, Vans posted the following statement on their website:

A NEW PAIR OF VANS CAN WAIT.

Today is Blackout Day, so before you spend money on our site, we ask that you consider shopping with your favorite Black-owned businesses or donating to organizations such as the NAACP, GSA Network, and Color of Change. Learn more about what we are doing to support Black Lives Matter and racial equality.

The statement wasn't in a corner of their website. It wasn't a banner at the top or a footnote at the bottom. That statement was the only thing you saw if you visited their page that day.

Making the Decision to Answer Your Why

If writing a statement isn't enough and you don't know where to start, you might be thinking you're damned if you do and damned if you don't. Instead, what you should be thinking is that you're damned if you don't have a strategy. One of the first questions I ask representatives from companies who have reached out to request unconscious bias education is "why?" Why do you want to offer this now? Why do you think this is the first course of action? Or the next step in a long list of actions that may have already been taken?

The answer is usually one of three things:

1. Silence, or we're not sure.
2. We started a DEI council and they decided we should have unconscious bias education.

3. Our employees expect us to do something because everyone else has done something and everyone is talking about unconscious bias, so we should tackle that.

Rarely is it something like this: "Our executive leaders wanted to know if we have adequately addressed unconscious bias in our workplace, so they tasked us with polling our workforce to determine where we should start. We conducted a survey that showed that many of our employees were concerned that bias may be to blame for some of the poor hiring decisions, lack of management diversity, and high turnover rates. We held a town hall to let our employees know the results of the survey and to inform them we are working on a strategy to address the findings."

Unconscious bias training is being used as a comfortable activity that is just enough of an action that it won't ruffle feathers.

Going back to May 24, 2020, it is quite likely that one of the following was accurate:

1. Diversity and inclusion was a high priority, and you were working on a strategy but there was no real sense of urgency.
2. Diversity and inclusion as a best practice or as a strategy was not on your list of high priorities.
3. Diversity and inclusion was not even on your radar.

Regardless of which of those is true, you were impacted by outside forces and your timeline and/or awareness was changed. You may not be happy about that impact, which is understandable. The perception may be that you are bowing to external pressure, but you're actually taking action that was needed previously and you ignored that need. Now you're rectifying that situation.

No one likes to be pushed before they are ready. It is similar to the stereotypical boyfriend who is given an ultimatum by his girlfriend: "It's marriage or nothing." In the case of the girlfriend who has waited only two years, the ultimatum may seem excessive. But in the case where the girlfriend has waited 15 years, everyone agrees the ultimatum probably should have occurred much sooner. The boyfriend may not like the ultimatum, but when faced with the very real possibility of living without this person in his life or doing something he now realizes is long overdue, he proposes.

In case you weren't aware, you're the boyfriend in the second scenario. You must decide what you stand for. Do you want to let your ego get in the way of doing what is right, or would you prefer to keep the status quo? You get to make that choice, but the problem is that *you* actually have to make that choice. Even if you're not the CEO, you have to enter your next meeting and demand that change happen, or you have to accept the fact that you plan to allow your workplace to continue operating as is. And to be clear, "as is" means any or all of the following:

- Unequal pay
- Sexual harassment at work
- No diversity in hiring
- A senior executive team that is all white and male
- High turnover
- Inability to attract diverse candidates to your company
- Job descriptions that continue to repel women from applying
- Toxic workplace culture
- No development opportunities for your employees
- Unclear goals and/or strategy
- Disengaged employees

Now you may think that is unfair. You may think you don't have these issues in your workplace. And my response would be, really? How would you know?

Unconscious bias education is not your starting point, and your employees do have expectations. It's the reason you wanted unconscious bias education to begin with. Why would your workforce think you need it if none of the above is occurring? Even if it was your diversity council that made the recommendation, regardless of who came to the conclusion education was needed, the decision didn't come out of nowhere. It stems from one or more of those workplace issues. So yes, you need unconscious bias education, but if you start there, you're putting the cart before the horse.

I mentioned before the importance of tying together your "why" for a diversity and inclusion strategy with your company's core values. In the next chapter, we will dig deeper into actually defining what those core values are.

3

What Is
Unconscious Bias?

Think about the last time you interviewed someone for a job. How did that go? Were you prepared for the interview well in advance, or did you scan their resume five minutes before they walked in the door?

Did you have a standard set of interview questions that you asked each candidate for the position, or did you ask ad hoc questions depending upon the candidate's response?

Were you in a rush to fill the position because it had been open for far too long?

Did you get a feeling about the person when they entered the room – did you immediately like or dislike someone based upon what they were wearing, the color of their hair, how long or short their nails were, the timbre of their voice, whether they had an accent? The list goes on and on.

Although I don't talk at length about the interviewing process until Chapter 11, you may notice throughout the book that I frequently use interviewing in my examples. This is because interviews are something that every person has had to endure at some point in their career and every leader has been tasked with doing it. Having been a recruiter for many years, I've seen that, for many companies, it is an area where unconscious bias education starts and stops.

Without even knowing it, recruiters and hiring managers may be exercising their unconscious biases, or those of their managers, through the process by which they screen and consider candidates. This is because our brains receive millions of pieces of information each second, a majority of which is processed by our brains at the unconscious level, effecting our decision-making, attitudes, and behaviors without our even knowing it.

A Tool for Unconsious Bias

Implicit bias as a concept was coined in the mid-'90s by psychologists Mahzarin Banaji and Anthony Greenwald. They made the assertion that social behavior is largely influenced by unconscious associations and judgments. With a consortium of researchers from Harvard University, the University of Virginia, and the University of Washington, they created the highly acclaimed and criticized Harvard Implicit Association Test (IAT), which offers a way to probe unconscious biases. The IAT is one of the most popular and well-known tools for individuals to use and was developed as part of a project to detect implicit or unconscious bias based on several factors including race, gender, sexual orientation, and national origin.

Measuring Attitudes and Beliefs

The IAT measures attitudes and beliefs that people may be unwilling or unable to report. Project Implicit notes that people don't always say what's on their minds. From their overview, they state that one reason could be that they are unwilling. For example, someone might report smoking a pack of cigarettes per day because they are embarrassed to admit that they actually smoke two packs per day. A second reason is that they are unable. A smoker might truly believe that she smokes one pack a day or might not keep track at all. The difference between being unwilling and unable is the difference between purposely hiding something from someone and unknowingly hiding something from yourself.

The IAT measures the relative strength of associations between pairs of concepts. By sorting words or images into categories, the tool measures the strength of the association by how quickly those concepts are paired. The order of the pairs changes and is shown in varying numbers of trials so to reduce the probability that you could repeatedly take the test and practice your way into a more acceptable outcome.

In a 2016 NPR interview, Banaji is quoted as follows:

In the late 1990s, I did a very simple experiment with Tony Greenwald in which I was to quickly associate dark-skinned faces – faces of black Americans – with negative words. I had to use a computer key whenever I saw a black face or a negative word, like devil or bomb, war, things like that. And likewise, there was another key on the keyboard that I had to strike whenever I saw a white face or a good word, a word like love, peace, joy. I was able to do this very easily. But when the test then switched the pairing and I had to use the same computer key to identify a black face with good things and white faces and bad things, my fingers appeared to be frozen on the keyboard. I literally could not find the right key. That experience is a humbling one. It is even a humiliating one because you come face to face with the fact that you are not the person you thought you were.[1]

The reliability and validity of the IAT has been rigorously tested, which is what makes this tool so widely used. However, as with anything, there are also detractors who argue that the test isn't ready for public use just yet. Some psychologists have also expressed concerns that individuals' scores could change from test to test, depending on their mood, making the results less definitive.

Using the Tool as a Conversation-Starter

With a normal test, the accuracy of the results would be a big deal. But this is not a math test. There isn't a 1+1 = 2 argument to be made here. In light of the framework that I have introduced and that I use with companies around the globe, the accuracy doesn't matter for what I believe is its intended purpose. I believe the intended purpose of the IAT is not to tell you how biased you are and to what degree. I believe the purpose of this test is to start a conversation, to get you thinking about the ways in which you interact with people who are different from you, and to spark action to behave more inclusively.

The IAT can be an effective awareness fielding tool, even if it isn't reliable as a scientific tool. Although, personally, I am not a huge fan of the test, if even half of the 17 million people who have taken it have changed their behavior as a result, then that's a great outcome. There are so few tools available that can actually measure

---

[1]https://www.npr.org/2016/10/17/498219482/how-the-concept-of-implicit-bias-came-into-being.

the presence or level of bias, so education efforts have mostly focused on increasing general self-awareness. (To take a look at the test, go to https://implicit.harvard.edu/implicit/takeatest.html.)

So, take the test. Draw your own conclusions and then start a conversation with others – not only individuals in your circle, but others outside of your network. Listen to people who may have a different perspective than you. Discuss the insights. What did you learn about yourself? How did you feel while taking it? Did you fear the outcome? Why or why not? Did you get the results you would expect?

Then take the Unconscious Bias course I created for LinkedIn Learning. My goal with the course was to encourage introspection and self-evaluation, but I also wanted people to understand that this concept of unconscious bias is universal. There aren't specific demographics of people who are more guilty of it than others. All of us could stand to be more self-aware in this area.

As is asserted by the creators of the IAT, the test is currently to be used for educational purposes only and as we've learned, education is only the beginning – we've got work to do.

My word of caution is that this is not a tool you can use to screen prospective employees, this is not a tool you should use to determine whether a promotion is warranted, and it cannot be used to decide who has greater ability to facilitate unconscious bias education.

Bias Comes in All Colors

Regardless of the criticisms or uses, unconscious bias still exists. Dismissing unconscious bias entirely because one test may have a flaw is an excuse that won't be tolerated.

You might assume – incorrectly, I might add – that if you're not white, you can't be biased. If you assumed that, you would be wrong for a number of reasons. First, not everything is about race and ethnicity. Second, there are many types of bias that exist among people of the same race and ethnicity. Some are social constructs, others stem from religion, and others come from plain old ignorance.

While unconscious bias may have been defined in the 1990's, more than 25 years later, we are still struggling with understanding the concept, let alone having the tools to begin to tackle it. It is one of the reasons I created an online course that addresses the concepts of unconscious bias. Partnering with LinkedIn, the course is available on the learning side of their platform and in less than 30 minutes, you are provided with examples, explanations, and the understanding that (1) you're not a bad person; (2) you're not alone in your assumptions; and (3) it's not only white people who have negative associations of Black people or men who have negative associations of women.

If you're left feeling, as Banaji states, as though you're not the person you thought you were, my course will help you back on the path to identifying and coming to terms with the person you want to be.

Quick Decisions Lead to Bias

Unconscious bias is defined as a way for us to quickly categorize other people without thinking. It is a shortcut our brains take that is affected by social, cultural, and religious norms. These shortcuts are the foundation of stereotypes and prejudice, and can lead to discrimination if we don't pay attention to the decisions we make without thinking. When we talk about bias, many of us have a bias and expectation that we are going to be talking about race and ethnicity, and that isn't always the case. There are actually more than 150 types of bias that focus on hair color, weight, where you live, accents, how tall you are, and much more.

Those biases can change depending upon social, cultural, and religious norms because they are based on the norms of your geographic area and your culture.

Remember when you were a child and your mother caught you doing something wrong? And before you even had a chance to explain she was dishing out a punishment? How did that make you feel? That she would just assume the broken vase, the hole in the carpet, or the missing item was your fault without missing a beat. Did it make you angry? Were you frustrated that she wouldn't even hear you out?

Unconscious bias can have that same effect. The word "bias" has a negative connotation. It assumes we are doing something wrong and doesn't give us the benefit of the doubt. And the act of being biased against someone does the same thing. The person on the receiving end of the bias is judged and decisions are made for that person before they ever get the opportunity to advocate for themselves.

Think about a new employee who we learn belonged to a fraternity in college. If we have the idea that individuals who joined a fraternity are more concerned about partying than work, the first time that employee comes to work late or doesn't meet a deadline, we say, yup, I knew it – party guy, lazy, slacker. And we ignore all the other days he came to work on time and met deadlines or went above and beyond in his job. We have identified and locked onto traits in a person that confirm the picture we've already created in our mind and that person is completely unaware that every day they are battling a mental picture of our own making.

Examples of bias are numerous. Have you ever crossed the street because you saw a group of boys walking your way or, clutched your purse because there was a Black man walking behind you? Did you ask John instead of Sue to go on a business trip because Sue has children or have you been Sue – wondering why you weren't given the opportunity?

Have you assumed Sanjeet was Muslim when he is actually Roman Catholic, skipped over a resume because the candidate's name was LaShawn and not Jane, or asked Sarah if she is bringing her husband to the party and then felt embarrassed when she showed up with Rebecca?

This is all due to us acting on our bias. As previously stated, the fact that we have a bias – many kinds of bias – doesn't make us bad people. But what we do with that bias very often has bad effects. This is what makes unconscious bias tricky.

Identify Bias to Make a Change

How are we supposed to battle a bias that is all encompassing and has the propensity to change based on social norms? And how do you address it when it shows up in your workplace?

The good news is, if unconscious bias occurs without us thinking about it, then by beginning to think consciously about our actions, we can stare it in the face, address it head on, and work together to minimize its effects.

You can't eradicate unconscious bias, but you can slow its appearance, you can identify it and name it when it happens, and then you can do something to lessen its impact. If unconscious bias is affected by social norms, then as a society, we can change what is '"normal"' and we can normalize treating others with dignity and respect.

Simply saying everyone has bias so why try to fix it is another excuse that won't be tolerated. So if you're looking for easy outs you should just throw this book in the trash and walk away now. As a leader in your company, it is your job to lead. If you're not up for the job, give the job to someone else – I don't mean delegate your responsibility, I mean leave your position. Being a leader is an active job with accountability and responsibility baked in.

If you're not up for the task, it's time to rethink your role in the company.

Values Are a Vital Place to Start

Let's be honest, there are other companies that already do what your company does, and they do it well. Your company's values are the only thing that differentiates your business. They're the piece of the puzzle that can impact decision-making for potential consumers.

In his book *Start with Why*, Sinek argues that people don't buy what you do, but rather *why* you do it. In the previous chapter we explored the '"why"' behind the decision to pursue unconscious bias training, but first you need to discern why your company exists at all or, as Sinek eloquently puts it, "Why do you get up in the morning, and why should anyone care?"

Finding My Why

Using my time at Prudential as an example, what did we stand for? Why did we exist? We didn't know, so we defaulted to making money as our answer and it is one of the reasons that we continued to have segregated teams and high turnover. However, my personal why – the reason I got up every day and continued to work in an industry that was sorely lacking in women and in representation by Black and Latino professionals – was to make a difference. I wanted to help people who hadn't historically had a financial advisor. I enjoyed seeing the happy surprise on the face of older Black individuals who failed to recognize when we spoke on the phone that I was Black. Remember what I said about assuming things about me? I was born in the UK so the way I spoke consistently confused people and thwarted their assumptions about me.

I had another "why" – to help more women take control of their finances and stop relying on their spouses to handle everything. I had seen too many heartbreaking stories of women over the age of 65 who had suddenly been left by a spouse with no home, no job, and no money. Having a 72-year-old woman sobbing in your office because she was a stay-at-home mom her whole life and is now destitute as a result of her divorce leaves an impression on you.

When I became a manager, my team was automatically diverse because I was intentional about my goals. We were diverse in race, ethnicity, socioeconomic status, gender, and geographic location. We were also successful. We were a top-performing team. Our team knew our individual whys. When advisors were having a tough day, a tough week, or even a tough month, they didn't quit, because they knew their why.

Finding Your Why

Companies that struggle with defining why their company exists often default to this answer: "To make money." The danger of this response is that it's actually a result, not a purpose, cause, or belief that drives the existence of your business. Others can't buy into your "why" if they don't know what it is or if it isn't more substantive than increased profit margins.

What your company does and *how* it does it are fairly simple things to conceptualize and communicate, but establishing *why* your company does what it does can be much more challenging, but don't be deterred. As American writer Dale Carnegie once said, "Inaction breeds doubt and fear [but] action breeds confidence and courage."

Your company's "why" should be embedded in its core values. As a leader, you have to stand for something, and your personal values should also align with your corporate values as a company. In a *Harvard Business Review* article, Patrick M. Lencioni, author of *The Five Dysfunctions of a Team*, said, "If you're not willing to accept the pain real values incur, don't bother going to the trouble of formulating a values statement. You'll be better off without one."[2] I couldn't agree more, which is why I quoted him. Consider this confirmation bias, I am partial to the *Cambridge Dictionary* definition of values: "The principles that help you to decide what is right and wrong, and how to act in various situations." What I like about it is that the action is baked right into the definition. Values aren't talk, they are action. They tell you how to *act*. That's a key part of your values and it is what is missing in so many companies.

Defining Values

Most of the following companies have multiple values, but I've randomly selected ones to include. Do these companies live up to their values?

- Zappos: Deliver WOW through service
- Pixar: People are more important than ideas
- Starbucks: Creating a culture of warmth and belonging, where everyone is welcome
- Apple: Accessibility
- Google: Focus on the user and all else will follow

During a consulting engagement, in an executive debrief meeting, the CEO of a tech company said, "We don't define values. We don't need them. Employees have to guide themselves."

---

[2]https://hbr.org/2002/07/make-your-values-mean-something.

It has been demonstrated that when you don't have well-defined, clear values, and your employees don't know what they are, decisions are difficult to make because employees don't know what matters to the company. Recruitment costs are high and so is turnover because it's tough to know if a person truly belongs at a company until they've had a chance to work there for a few months.

If you're unsure of what your company values are, there are thousands of resources available to help you identify what's most important to your business. A simple way to kickstart the process would be to ask your employees:

- Why does our company exist?
- Who do we serve and why are we good at what we do?
- From your experience, what does our company value?

Once you've collected responses from your employees, move on to your executive team. Are there responses that show up more than once? These are good indicators of what your company values most and can help you in crafting a values statement.

The purpose of a values statement, at least as it relates to diversity and inclusion, is that it draws a line in the sand. It makes it clear what is, and what is not acceptable in the workplace. When adhered to, it makes leaders accountable along with everyone else. When leaders model behaviors of an inclusive workplace, employees know what is expected of them. If you avoid responsibility and ignore the need for clear values, the list of status quo behaviors remains. As a reminder, some of those include:

- Unequal pay
- Sexual harassment at work
- No diversity in hiring

- A senior executive team that is all white and male
- High turnover
- Inability to attract diverse candidates to your company
- Job descriptions that continue to repel women from applying
- Toxic workplace culture
- No development opportunities for your employees
- Unclear goals and/or strategy
- Disengaged employees

If you're a little uncomfortable, I hope that you're not hopeless. My intent is to be the grain of sand that gets into your shoe and you stop at nothing to get it out. I'd like you to feel the same way about bias, inequity, and lack of belonging in your workplace.

Feeling Uncomfortable Fosters Change

The importance of this can't be overstated. One of my prior clients is a tech company with about 500 employees. They are a privately held company with an executive team of twelve, ten of whom are white men. There is one Black man and one woman. Prior to my consulting engagement, they established a DEI council and we decided to have an education session so that I could learn more about their challenges, understand the direction they were moving toward, and begin to formulate education sessions for the entire company. When we started the session, everyone was in a good mood. They were feeling optimistic about their plans and were excited to discuss the challenges they were facing. By the end of the session, everyone's mood had shifted. I polled the group because I could sense the mood shift and nearly everyone was feeling upset, hopeless, and bordering on a mentality of "why bother?" This mood shift was caused by the realization that a lot of work needed to be done in the company and they had zero faith that their CEO would change his attitude. He was at the core of many of the issues that employees were experiencing and it was the first time that reality had hit them in the face. It was quite sobering.

We were able to work through it, but I mention this example to implore you not to be *that* leader. Don't be a cautionary tale. Instead, be a shining example, because unconscious bias may be a complex problem, but addressing it doesn't require a complex solution.

4

Leaders Lead Teams Who Trust

Have you ever felt uncomfortable sharing your opinion, asking questions, or making mistakes?

Do you know if your employees feel comfortable sharing their opinion in your company? Can they ask for help without being viewed as incompetent? Can they take risks that won't be held against them if they fail? According to Gallup, only three out of ten employees in the United States strongly agree that their opinions count at work. People hold back because they don't feel safe to engage.

Creating Comfort Through Pyschological Safety

There are so many nuances to unconscious bias in the workplace and without psychological safety, you cannot hope to address them. For example, if you are in a meeting and the only woman on the team comes into the conference room and sits on the outskirts of the room, do you invite her into the inner circle and encourage her to participate in the meeting, or do you assume she is only there to take notes and say nothing?

Assuming you didn't notice the difference in seating, psychological safety allows someone else within the meeting to feel comfortable in speaking up and addressing the situation if they notice it.

Encourage Open Communication

Psychological safety allows team members to feel safe to take risks and to be vulnerable with one another. The term was coined by Dr. Amy Edmondson, who defines it as "a climate in which people are comfortable being (and expressing) themselves. Dr. Edmondson is a Harvard Business School professor and she researched different teams and their effectiveness. Her data showed that teams who performed better were communicating more openly about making mistakes.

We all make mistakes, but as Henry Ford said, "The only real mistake is the one from which we learn nothing." In an organization where you can learn not only from your own mistakes but also from the mistakes of others, you can innovate more rapidly. In teams that encourage discussing mistakes, you prevent others from making the same mistake and accelerate learning much more quickly. Take the example of Kim Malone, who worked as the director of the AdSense Ops team at Google. She encouraged the sharing of mistakes that were made that week and would award "Whoops" (a stuffed monkey) to the winner – the person with the worst mistake, as voted on by their 75-member team. Whoops helped Kim to create a culture where sharing mistakes was normal, where transparency was expected, and where learning was valued.[1]

This open communication allows for effective performers to learn from their failures. With failure and mistakes as part of experimentation, this promotes learning and allows for everyone to improve collectively.

Encouraging everyone to share and avoiding blame or punishment sets the stage to allow for experimentation, to discuss the mistakes, be open to new ideas, and reflect on how things can be done differently in the future.

What Happens When Dialogue Is Discouraged?

I previously worked for a video game company where we put out some of the best games in the world. Unfortunately, we also put out some of the worst games in the world. Some of that could've been avoided had we had psychological safety in our teams. I vividly recall being in a greenlight meeting discussing a title that everyone had been talking about for weeks. It was a reboot of an old title that had failed the first time. We couldn't understand why the VP was insistent that this time it would be a hit. We all thought it was terrible; the game was past its time and no one was clamoring for this reboot.

However, in that meeting, no one mentioned any of the criticisms we had been discussing for weeks and no one brought up any of the concerns about viability. We all sat silently as the VP talked about how great this title would be, how much revenue

---

[1]https://tomtunguz.com/a-dog-and-a-monkey.

we would make, and how excited he was to move forward with the project.

The game was a major flop, and the VP was the only person who was surprised by this fact. The company lost hundreds of thousands of dollars and was the laughingstock of the video game community for many months.

Why did no one speak up? Because we had all learned that our ideas were no good in these meetings. We learned that our opinions were not respected and that it was best not to open our mouths unless it was to agree. We understood that the creative VPs believed they had a monopoly on ideas, and we watched as new employees came in, attempted to provide feedback, and were very soon thereafter let go. We stopped bothering to share our thoughts because it was futile.

Free Contribution Equals Success

An internal study conducted by Google found that teams with high rates of psychological safety were better than other teams at implementing diverse ideas and driving high performance. Rates of retention with the company were also higher. By improving the Gallup ratio from three out of ten to six out of ten employees who feel their opinions count at work, turnover was reduced by 27%, safety incidents were reduced by 40%, and productivity increased by 12%.

Fostering a climate where employees feel free to contribute ideas, share information, and report mistakes is vital to company success. Psychological safety is not about being nice. It is actually dependent on there being a level of healthy conflict in the workplace. But that conflict can only arise when employees know it is safe to say the hard thing, bring up the uncomfortable conversation, or present the point of view that some may not want to hear.

Trust Is Essential

Psychological safety is also not the same as trust, although you can't have psychological safety without trust and vice versa. Anders Wendelheim developed the openness and trust spiral (see Figure 4.1),[2] a simple concept that can easily be continued without much effort. But when broken, it can be difficult to repair. The feedback loop requires a little vulnerability, which sparks the beginning of trust between group members. By being open, trust is formed. By knowing you can trust one another, you are able to be more open without fear of being rejected or shamed.

Create Group Norms to Foster Belonging

Pixar Studios is known for their creative and innovative movie-making magic and much of that can be credited to their efforts to create psychological safety at work. In a *Harvard Business Review* article titled, "How Pixar Fosters Collective Creativity," Ed Catmull, cofounder of Pixar, explained the principles they adhere to:

1. Everyone must have the freedom to communicate with anyone.

2. It must be safe to offer ideas.

3. We must stay close to innovations happening in the academic community.

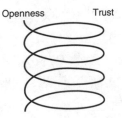

FIGURE 4.1 The Openness and Trust Spiral.
Source: Based on The Core Team, Anders Wendelheim, Senior Consultant and Partner, Core Consulting Group.

---

[2]http://www.corecg.com/swe/wendelheim.htm.

These principles demonstrate they really mean it when they say people are more important than ideas, no idea is more important simply because it comes from someone with more seniority, and no one will be penalized for criticizing a good idea or offering a bad one.[3]

What Pixar consistently demonstrates is the concept of group norms, which are informal guidelines that give structure to group activities. After looking at more than 100 teams for over a year, project Aristotle researchers at Google homed in on the research they uncovered by psychologists and sociologists that focused on group norms.

"Norms are the traditions, behavioral standards and unwritten rules that govern how we function when we gather: . . . Team members may behave in certain ways as individuals . . . but when they gather, the group's norms typically override individual proclivities and encourage deference to the team."[4]

Why are group norms so important? If you recall, unconscious bias is affected by social norms and so by creating group norms, you are using psychological safety as one way to address unconscious bias at work. You effectively create a new way of thinking and create a new, positive way of interacting that includes everyone, rather than marginalizing or excluding. Group norms also create a sense of belonging for the individuals of that team so by increasing psychological safety, you address unconscious bias, create inclusion, and foster a sense of belonging.

By demonstrating that the team is a safe space for risk taking, the members of that team can go beyond interpersonal trust and establish a level of confidence that creates inclusion and sparks innovation.

---

[3]https://hbr.org/2008/09/how-pixar-fosters-collective-creativity.
[4]https://www.nytimes.com/2016/02/28/magazine/what-google-learned-from-its-quest-to-build-the-perfect-team.html.

Psychological safety means you have fostered an environment where employees feel included, have a safe space to learn, are safe to contribute their ideas, and are safe to disagree or challenge the status quo. Safety means they can do these things without fear of retribution, shame, or being ostracized. You have to model psychological safety, and this requires doing the following:

- Ensure you have contributions from everyone and are not simply listening to the loudest voices.
- Encourage the contribution of ideas by demonstrating listening and that ideas won't be dismissed.
- Expect disagreement and valuing challenges to the status quo, and not having people say things like "We've always done it this way."
- Remain curious and open to alternative solutions rather than assuming you have the right, the best, or the only answer.

Psychological safety is not all you need to foster high performance among diverse teams. But you can't have high performance without diverse teams. Psychological safety gives permission for exploration along the path of your journey to an inclusive workplace. It removes some of the barriers that keep people from achieving what is possible.

Trust Is Essential

Do you trust your team? Does your team trust you? One way to improve psychological safety in your workplace is to encourage everyone to speak up. Teams are becoming more diverse, which means intercultural communication is also a factor. Some cultures teach women not to be opinionated or to offer an opinion that is contrary to someone who is older than they are.

Others are simply shy and have a hard time speaking up. Accounting for those who are visual and need to see what's being discussed prior to talking about it, encouraging everyone to write on an index card will ensure you receive feedback from everyone, not just the loudest voices. It gives everyone a chance to ask questions, share concerns, or provide additional ideas that may otherwise have been overlooked.

If you aren't already doing these things, try implementing one at a time:

- Start meetings with a way to connect. Learn more about your team. Ask them how they are feeling and be genuine in your response.
- Be vulnerable. As leaders, we come to work and think our private life is separate from our work life, but work has changed and people want to see you as a person too, not just a leader. Share something about you that makes you personable.
- Ask for opinions and feedback, and not only in a one-on-one or in a performance management meeting, but randomly check in to learn how your team is collaborating.

Trust also gets built by how you react to mistakes. Humans are inherently mistrustful and our minds always stray to the negative outcome. Don't believe me? If your supervisor asks you to join them in their office, your first thought is probably "What did I do wrong?" You're definitely not thinking, "I'm about to get a raise or a promotion." Building trust is important, but avoiding ways in which you can erode trust is just as vital. When a comment is misconstrued, it's always spun into a negative light, never the positive.

So if someone is frustrated or angry with you, rather than get defensive, remember that they probably misconstrued your intentions and it's your job to get your point across in a positive way.

- Difficult communications shouldn't be had by email, where you can't properly convey tone.
- Difficult conversations also shouldn't be had when you're angry or upset with a team member. When in doubt, use another member of the team as a sounding board. Gauge their opinion and obtain feedback.
- Do the same for written communications. Check with someone else before you send out a communication that may not be received well.

We all make mistakes, but whether trust will be built or destroyed depends upon how we own those mistakes and learn from them as leaders.

2

Alignment

5

Why Diversity?
Why Now?

Diversity is a "must-have," not a "nice-to-have." It is a require-ment for businesses to continue to thrive. Inevitably, your mind wanders to the companies who are doing well, the compa-nies that the public believes don't need to worry about tackling diversity because there is high demand for their products and people just love them.

Let's identify those companies: Google, Starbucks, Apple, Pixar, Amazon, Netflix – you get the idea. Whether you enjoy the products they sell, like the values they stand for, or agree with their business practices, the facts are that these companies are thriving. Despite their profitability and high reputation in the marketplace, these companies are still concerned with diversity.

Google (Alphabet, Inc.) is a Fortune Best Company to Work For and has landed the top spot as *the* number one Best Company to Work For many years in a row. Analysts recommend their stock as one to buy, and according to Glassdoor.com, 90% of employees would recommend working there to a friend, while 94% of employees approve of the CEO. Despite their high industry and employee rating, high profitability, and innovation, in an interview Alphabet CEO Sundar Pichai is quoted as saying, "Diversity is a foundational value for us."[1]

Starbucks is the only other company I mentioned that consistently makes it to the Fortune Best Company to Work For list. Despite this, Apple's CEO, Tim Cook, said, "I think the most diverse group will produce the best product, I firmly believe that," when asked about diversity in an interview with Mashable.[2] And employees agree, with 83% of employees recommending working at Apple to a friend and a 93% approval rating of the CEO, according to Glassdoor.com.

As I was writing this book, Amazon provided an example of a way in which they embrace diversity. On September 20, 2020, an Amazon employee posted the following to her LinkedIn profile:

What began as a simple conversation with my manager turned into a major win at my FC [Fulfillment Center] site. As an expectant mother at almost 8 months pregnant, I was finding it increasingly difficult to trek through our large parking lot each day, so I brought it up to her. As a result of our conversation, it was brought to the attention of several members of our Sr. Site Leadership team and the outcome was the

---

[1] https://www.theverge.com/2020/5/19/21262934/google-alphabet-ceo-sundar-pichai-interview-pandemic-coronavirus.
[2] https://mashable.com/2015/06/08/tim-cook-apple-diversity-women-future/.

approval to add several expectant mother parking spaces to the front of our parking lot. Though it may seem small to many, this was a major win to me and one that I hope can be considered at other sites as well. Very grateful to be part of a company who listens to feedback from its associates and actually practices the leadership principles on which our business is run.

At first glance you may think this has nothing to do with diversity, but this is why seeing diversity as a separate issue from employee engagement is harmful. If I told you the pregnant employee was Black, would it then become a diversity issue for you? Diversity at work isn't just about race, ethnicity, and gender; it's about creating a place where the employees you have hired are included and feel they belong so they can be productive in the job you have hired them to do.

Creating a Diverse Workforce

Embracing diversity starts by actually encouraging a diverse workforce. In the case of the pregnant employee at Amazon who mentioned a concern she was having: (1) she felt comfortable letting someone know; (2) someone actually listened; and (3) someone did something about it. You can't begin to manage the various situations that will arise when you have a diverse workforce if you don't actually have a diverse workforce. Yes, you will have to decide how to handle the employee who has purple hair in the workplace, the employee who has a face tattoo, or a nonbinary employee who doesn't use the pronouns he or she. You'll also realize your conference meeting rooms don't properly meet the needs of your employee in a wheelchair or that some of your employees have been struggling with a mental health concern that can be helped by including an Employee Assistance Program as one of your employee benefits.

But managing a diverse workforce isn't always about the in-your-face diversity you can see. It's about tacking the unconscious biases that cloud your judgment and affect your actions. Reuters reported that the CEO of Wells Fargo wrote in a June 18, 2020, memo, "While it might sound like an excuse, the unfortunate reality is that there is a very limited pool of black talent to recruit from." Charles Scharf, the author of the quote, reiterated that message during a virtual meeting later that summer.[3]

The point here isn't about the calls to boycott Wells Fargo, because that was a very real possibility, nor is the point about the negative publicity this company received as a result. The point here is about the unconscious bias of this high-level executive that affects recruitment practices, advancement policies, and hiring procedures. When you make the claim that finding diverse talent is difficult or that Black talent are like unicorns, you make them stand out in the process, which inadvertently reinforces the notion that they are somehow special or different and makes them less likely to be hired.

No one likes to go against the status quo, so if you think that having at least one diverse candidate in the pool is a good thing, you might be surprised to know that *Harvard Business Review* has cited studies demonstrating that if there is only one woman in your candidate pool, there is statistically no chance she will be hired.[4]

If there are at least two female candidates in the final candidate pool, the odds of hiring a female candidate are 79 times

---

[3]https://www.businessinsider.com/exclusive-wells-fargo-ceo-ruffles-feathers-with-comments-about-diverse-talent-2020-9.
[4]https://hbr.org/2016/04/if-theres-only-one-woman-in-your-candidate-pool-theres-statistically-no-chance-shell-be-hired.

greater and when there are least two minority candidates in the final candidate pool the odds of hiring a minority candidate are 194 times greater.

Looking at Case Alignment

When determining why diversity might be important, companies will look at one of three things: the compliance or legal case, the moral case, and the business case:

- **Legal case:** When companies focus on the legal case, they are concerned with not getting sued. They want to ensure they have done the minimum necessary to avoid a lawsuit or to avoid a fine. This requires the human resources department to stay focused on compliance. They want to ensure they are up to date on all of the new laws and regulations and that employee handbooks, policies, and procedures are in line with whatever those legal and industry standards are.

- **Moral case:** Companies that focus on the moral case believe it is the right thing to do and will take a principled stance that makes it clear they believe this. As an example, Salesforce invested millions to audit employee compensation and worked to close their gender pay gap. They publicized their findings, and they publicized their action.

- **Business case:** The business case is where many companies will focus because it is easy to explain the appeal. Who doesn't want to increase business profitability and innovation? It allows companies to focus on the business aspects without having to seem as though they are touching on areas of society they have no business dealing in. While the legal case for diversity is viewed as authoritarian and reeks of too much oversight, the business case allows companies to set their own rules and standards. However, there is research to show that there is value in focusing on antidiscrimination laws as the most effective way to address unconscious bias and promote inclusion in the workplace.[5]

Legal Case: Following the Laws

I wholeheartedly believe you need to have all three aligned in a company. Maintaining focus on these aspects is not an either/or scenario, instead, it's both. The Civil Rights Act of 1964 was enacted to prohibit discrimination on the basis of race, color, religion, sex, or national origin. Provisions of this act forbade discrimination on the basis of sex, as well as race, in hiring, promoting, and firing, and prohibited discrimination in public accommodations and federally funded programs. It also strengthened the enforcement of voting rights and the desegregation of schools. Therefore, when diversity initiatives first began, they were merely a reaction to the requirements of this act. Companies focused on diversity to make sure they were in compliance.

But if you consider sexual harassment as an example, simply ensuring that handbooks and policies speak to the letter of the law is not enough. When you don't have a culture that encourages people to behave in accordance with the laws and actively speak up when people don't behave in accordance with the laws, you have a lot of policies that simply have no teeth to them.

And on the discussion of policies, please note that on June 15, 2020, the Supreme Court of the United States held that an employer that "fires an individual merely for being gay or transgender violates Title VII of the Civil Rights Act of 1964."

---

[5]https://scholarship.law.georgetown.edu/facpub/1961/.

If your policies do not already prohibit discrimination based on sexual orientation and gender identity, it is past time to update them.

Other policies that are important to your employees include dress codes and grooming policies. Many companies, from FedEx to Disney, have instituted dress codes under the premise that they are private entities and have the right to dictate how an employee dresses or appears at work, but I'm going to pick on Six Flags because when it comes to discriminating against hairstyles, they seem to do it with ease. On their application, Six Flags used to require that employee check "Yes" or "No" to the following question:

Our dress code strictly prohibits facial jewelry (other than 1 earring per earlobe for females only), extreme haircuts and colors, and visible tattoos. Are you willing and able to adhere to this dress code policy or do you believe you would qualify for a religious accommodation which might exempt you?

Between 2006 and 2019, Six Flags has had complaints and lawsuits filed against them for acts specifically relating to discriminating with regard to their dress code policy in several states. The CROWN Act was signed into law in the state of California in July 2019 specifically to address this pervasive problem. The Creating a Respectful and Open Workplace for Natural Hair (CROWN) Act has been duplicated and a form of it has been enacted in the states of New York, New Jersey, Virginia, Colorado, and Washington while a similar bill was introduced to Congress. As of September 21, 2020, the bill passed the House Judiciary Committee and was sent to the Senate Committee on the Judiciary for review and action.

The reason compliance as a diversity initiative doesn't work is because you shouldn't have to wait for the government to tell you to give rights to your employees that are simply common sense. Just because there isn't a law about it, doesn't mean you can't address it in your workplace today.

It can be easier to understand the concept when using physical safety as an example. In October 2010, B.O.S.S. Construction was cited by the U.S. Department of Labor's Occupational Safety and Health Administration (OSHA) for failing to provide hard hats to their employees. In a news release, they stated, "Falling is the great safety hazard for workers on roofing projects, and B.O.S.S. Construction has demonstrated a pattern of disregard for its workers' safety." Do you really have to wait until a law is passed or an administrative rule is created to make you do what is right and clearly in the best interests of your employees?

Moral Case: Being Right Isn't Enough

A second reason that companies will decide they need to tackle diversity is because it's simply the right thing to do. And while that is accurate, and admirable, it isn't sustainable. When you operate from the perspective that it's the right thing to do, the "right thing" is usually being championed by one lone individual or a small group without a lot of influence. Leaders change, budgets shrink, and priorities shift.

In 2015, in an effort to start a national dialogue about the deaths of Michael Brown and Eric Garner, two unarmed Black men, Howard Schultz, former CEO of Starbucks, came up with the "Race Together" campaign.

What if we were to write race together on every Starbucks cup, and that facilitated a conversation between you and our customers? . . . If a customer asks you what this is, try to engage in a discussion.

—*Howard Schutz, CEO, Starbucks*

While the campaign was short-lived, poorly organized, and ill-contrived, he pushed the envelope because he could. He was the CEO. But what happens when you're no longer focused on the moral case for diversity? One of your employees in Philadelphia calls the police on two Black men and you spark a national dialogue about racial profiling, that's what happens.

Operating on the premise that diversity is the right thing to do isn't sustainable because if it is a pet project of one or two leaders and is not embraced by everyone, when that leader leaves the company, so does the idea that diversity matters. This reinforces the need for grasping data and an understanding of where the organization as a whole stands on the issues, tying diversity to values and aligning leaders collectively, before moving to action.

Business Case: The Bottom Line

Third, there is the business case for diversity. This has been studied and analyzed by McKinsey, Deloitte, and *Harvard Business Review*, just to name a few.

Boston Consulting Group conducted a study that demonstrated that 19% higher revenues are earned in companies that are more diverse. *Harvard Business Review* has conducted numerous studies showing that diverse companies are 70% more likely to capture new markets. McKinsey's research indicates that when it comes to outperforming peer companies, gender-diverse companies are 15% more likely to outperform and ethnically diverse companies are 35% more likely to outperform.[6] Bersin by Deloitte has also reported that after surveying and interviewing 450 global companies, companies they labeled "inclusive" had 2.3 times higher cash flow per employee over a three-year period.

---

[6]https://www.mckinsey.com/~/media/mckinsey/business%20functions/organization/our%20insights/why%20diversity%20matters/diversity%20matters.ashx.

Experts agree, businesses that are more diverse are more profitable and if you refer to a SWOT (Strengths, Weaknesses, Opportunities, and Threats) analysis, this would fall solidly under "strengths" if you are already embracing diversity and incorporating it as a value. But if you're not there yet, then it will fall in the "opportunities" category.

A great example of leveraging diversity is Hallmark. When they were having trouble selling their cards in a particular retail store location, they tried everything to improve revenues. The store was getting ready to terminate the relationship and remove their cards from the location, but Hallmark requested additional time to resolve the issue and conducted a demographic study of the neighborhood.

When the results of the survey indicated that the community immediately surrounding the retail store location had a high LGBTQ population, they took their lagging sales problem to their LGBTQ Employee Resource Group. A subset of their ERG (Employee Resource Group) visited the retail store location and diagnosed what they believed the problem to be. They concluded that the imagery, the labels, and the overall branding of the entire card aisle needed redesigning.

They worked with the marketing team, the team that writes the content inside the cards, and the graphic designers to create cards that were inclusive of LGBTQ families. No longer were the aisle labels strictly for moms, dads, husbands, and wives. Instead those labels were changed to use more inclusive terms such as spouse, partner, parent, and caregiver.

Without the diversity of their employee population, they would have been unable to resolve this issue so quickly and maintain the revenue from that retail store location. In addition, not only did they maintain the revenue, but they increased revenue until they were the best-performing store in that region.

Demonstrate Desire to Change Through Transparency

While revenue is great, you also would like to avoid appearing as though you care more about the company bottom line than the customers you serve or the employees who create your products. There may be individuals in your company who are wondering why it has taken you so long to come to the conclusion that diversity and inclusion needed to be tackled in the workplace because they work there and it personally affects them every single day. They wonder if you couldn't see this previously as a human relations issue, then maybe you'll see it as a business imperative. This is where it is important to be authentic as a leader. You may now see diversity and inclusion as a strategic imperative, or you may see it as a human rights issue and realize it's the right thing to do. Regardless of the reason, you have to demonstrate that you plan to do something about this and really mean it.

Remember the CEO of the tech company I mentioned previously (see Chapter 3)? What I didn't tell you is that nobody wanted him at their town hall meeting. Authenticity and transparency are vital as you go through change, and frequent communication with employees is necessary. As you get started on this journey, you have to explain to your workforce why you're on this journey, what the destination is, and how bumpy the road may be along the way. You also need to give them a roadmap to follow so they can all make it to the destination together. Not wanting your CEO at the town hall meeting is a big deal. It is a huge red flag and we spent many months partnering with the DEI council, the executive leaders, and the CEO to unravel their problems and challenge perceptions.

On the subject of transparency, a town hall is a great vehicle to demonstrate authenticity and offer transparency to your workforce. With my clients I use a town hall as a communication tool to reach large numbers of employees all at once. Town halls serve as flexible containers for adding in many types of communication styles. You can host a panel with curated questions being answered by the heads of specific departments, you can host a fireside chat with the CEO, or you can prerecord messages from various key personnel and include them prior to the live message.

There are companies who are concerned about hosting a town hall because they worry about what individuals might say. That is a huge, waving red flag that tells you there are problems to be addressed. It can be scary and you may uncover things you don't want to hear, but unpleasant realities have a way of coming out without regard to whether we want to know. Address them anyway.

Don't think communication is important to your workforce? Consider that 85% of employees say they're most motivated when management offers regular updates on company news.[7] Even more astounding, in a pulse survey by Perceptyx, an employee survey and people analytics company, when employees are extremely satisfied with communications about the company's response to the coronavirus, 96% of them believe that their employer really puts their safety first. When communication is poor, only 62% of them believe so. The difference communication makes is quite noticeable.[8]

Combining the three "cases" for diversity will set you on a path to addressing the biased behavior that puts up barriers to action.

---

[7]https://www.tradepressservices.com/internal-communications/.
[8]https://blog.perceptyx.com/covid-19-insights-what-employees-need-from-leaders?utm_campaign=Monthly%20Insights%20Newsletter).

Why diversity? Why now? If the workforce doesn't understand why the company is moving in the direction that it is, it could be a direct result of the failure to communicate the value. If there is no transparency in leadership, the motives will be in doubt. A study by IBM found that 72% of employees don't understand their company's strategy, and in my work with organizations I've found that is largely due to a lack of communication. Employees can't understand what they don't know about. Subsequently layering unconscious bias education on top of authentic communications will begin to open up the discussions that are necessary, create awareness of the issues, and generate the impact desired by company leadership.

6

Diversity Is
in the Data

Now that we've discussed why your company should tackle its diversity and inclusion issues, as well as the importance of open and honest communication from the top down, it's time to touch base with your employees to collect some hard data. If you're hoping to cultivate a change in earnest, you have to listen to the experiences of the people who interface with your work culture every day. It has been said that you can't fix what you won't face, and this kind of data will help you face what needs fixing.

When it comes to collecting data from your employees, a number of tools are available. It may help to start by considering feedback channels your employees are already familiar with. What have you done in the past to measure things like employee engagement, job satisfaction, or brand awareness? How effective were the tools you used?

Maybe your company has never attempted to collect feedback from its employees. If this is true for you, know that you're not alone. Leaders of companies large and small have shied away from the feedback loop for various reasons.

Some avoid using surveys because they believe that conducting one will stir up issues and cause problems that could have been left alone. They wonder why people can't just let sleeping dogs lie. The thing about sleeping dogs is that eventually they wake up. Conducting the survey doesn't cause issues, but not conducting a survey allows issues to remain undetected until one day they are uncovered by a plaintiff's attorney.

Leaders who are reluctant to gather data have the perception that, if they ask questions, employees will assume something is wrong. When I assist companies by performing one-on-one interviews with their staff, I always begin by informing the employee that there isn't a lawsuit, no one has been fired, and there isn't any wrongdoing that we're aware of, but we're conducting these interviews so that it hopefully stays that way.

Reluctance also stems from denial. Any leader worth their salt usually has an inkling that things aren't quite right. They know the culture could be improved and they know when something is wrong. But if they ask questions, they will actually have to do something about it, so it's easier to pretend that everything is fine. Unfortunately, some leaders are just plain unaware. They don't think anything is wrong because they are blissfully disengaged. Since they are blind to the goings on in the company, they haven't even thought about asking questions – it's just not on their radar.

Define What You're Measuring

Assuming you're not in denial or unaware, I hope you see that as you work to create a baseline for action, data gathering is necessary to guide you in creating a strategy. Data also helps you make the case for your strategy by providing you with backup for your intended actions.

Before going into detail about different ways to collect data, it's important to specifically pinpoint the information you want to collect. When it comes to issues of diversity, nailing down one definition of the term can prove challenging. For example, as a diversity and inclusion practitioner, a DEI consultant, or even a diversity strategist, you can see that just position titles alone can cause a person to focus on one aspect of diversity over another. When you use the word "diversity," what do you mean? Are you speaking from the literal view by which diversity means different, or are you speaking more specifically, such as non-male and non-white? Leaving a broad term like "diversity" undefined is detrimental to the accuracy of the information you're trying to gather. From the outset, clearly define what it is you're measuring. As you set out to collect the data, whether it be through a survey, interviews, focus groups, or a town hall meeting, ensure that those you are gathering information from also understand that definition.

After clearly defining what it is you want to measure, establish what your goal will be with the results. What are you ultimately attempting to learn? After all, conducting a survey is a great idea, but only if you actually intend to do something about the results. As we move into specifics about data collecting strategies, remember that, regardless of the ultimate actions your company takes to address its diversity issues, you will have both naysayers and promoters, so you will need to have sound reasoning to explain the changes you made and why you made them. That sound reasoning will come directly from data, so choose your feedback channel wisely. The "why," as discussed in Chapters 2 and 3, should come from your values.

Three Forms of Data Collection

It is apparent that employees don't actually have an issue with giving feedback. They want to give feedback. If you'll recall, according to Gallup, only three out of ten employees in the United States strongly agree that their opinions count at work and when that number increased to six out of ten, employee engagement increased. They want their opinions to count, but what employees take issue with is the lack of outcome. There is an expectation that if their company is going to take the time and spend the amount of money they do on surveying, interviewing, or using focus groups with their workforce, that at the end of it, something positive will occur or that things might change for the better. They expect that if leadership is going to take the time to ask for their opinion, they should actually act upon it.

Surveys, interviews, and focus groups are three inexpensive ways to begin to understand your workplace culture:

- **Surveys:** Surveys are a great way to obtain data from a large number of people in different geographic locations, across offices, and across roles and titles. Technology makes data collection and analyzing much simpler, faster, and more accurate today than has been in the past. Surveys are also a great tool for finding nuance in the data. Everyone wants Christmas as a vacation day, right? Well, maybe not. Do you know the religion of your employees?

  Even well-intentioned executive decisions may fall flat because they don't take into account the actual needs and priorities of the people those decisions affect. For example, let's say a committee in downtown San Francisco is fighting to bring broadband internet to a small Cambodian neighborhood; however, the committee is made up of six white males. While it is true that the neighborhood may need broadband, they actually have a greater need for more access to public transportation or addressing sanitation concerns.

Ultimately, you can't know what your employees need or care about until you ask them. Surveys are an efficient and effective way to do just that.

- **Interviews:** While surveys can gather lots of data from many different people, individual interviews are used to pinpoint issues that may be arising by having a much deeper conversation. Those conversations can help point you in a direction you may need to explore, as well as inform the content of future surveys and/or education or professional development that may be needed as a result. They can also be anonymous and really get to the heart of delicate situations that may be occurring.

- **Focus groups or group forums:** These have their use as a way to speak with a larger number of individuals than with interviews, but you still will not be able to reach as many people as you can with a survey. One of the reasons to use this type of data-gathering tool is to gain more insight than you can in a survey. It offers the opportunity for two-way communication.

- **Town hall meetings:** Companies can use these meetings to reach all of their employees. It's a good way to connect and find out how employees are feeling on certain issues.

I want to make it clear that things don't have to be wrong for any of these tools to be put into action. If things are going well, you want to know that too so you can do more of it and replicate it throughout your entire company.

Starting with Surveys

Company representatives that reach out and request unconscious bias education will usually say they don't need to do surveys because they don't have a problem in their workplace, and they know this because no one has said anything. In a company of 200 or even 2,000, no one at all has said anything? When I hear this, I make the assumption that no one has said anything because they know it would fall on deaf ears, or alternatively, it's because they don't have a process in place to obtain that feedback.

Surveys are one of the most popular processes to collect feedback because they allow for data gathering from a large group of individuals with a fast response time. However, I am surprised by the number of employers I have met with that have not surveyed their employees recently or at all. In the example where most companies now want to offer unconscious bias education, I believe it is important to ask employees what they think about and I'm usually met with blank stares when I say this. Why is it such a foreign concept to ask your employees their opinions and thoughts about what is occurring in the workplace?

Most employees have thought long and hard about how they can improve working conditions and they would know because they are tasked with doing the very job you hired them for. They also observe behaviors every single day. They know what is working and what isn't. Or they at least have some very strong opinions about it.

Anonymity in surveys is vitally important. I see this repeatedly with companies who have low response rates on surveys. They said their employees aren't engaged or they don't care, but once we start digging into company culture and learning about how their company works, we learn there are trust issues – lots of them. In tech companies, employees believe their senior leaders who are tech savvy will reverse engineer the survey to learn who said what and use that information against them. Other concerns I've seen include sample sizes – when offices are small, employees believe they can be identified by their office location and one of the demographics, and they're not wrong. But there are ways to handle these concerns while obtaining the necessary data and still maintaining anonymity.

The simplest way to collect information while protecting employee anonymity is to hire a third party to develop/administer surveys or perform one-on-one interviews. These independent teams are able to generalize sentiments so that the gist of the issue is presented without any unnecessary, identifiable details. For example, "There's a general feeling that minorities working for the company feel this way."

Whether you go outside of the company or keep the assessment in-house, there are ways to utilize filters when looking at your data to protect individual identities. You can turn off specific categories that may not be necessary in identifying your company's specific issues. Using the example from the previous paragraph, you could turn off the gender and age categories and still convey the message that minorities don't feel as though they belong. Likewise, you could turn off the race and gender categories and still convey that your older employees are feeling undervalued.

Ultimately, whomever you choose to compile the necessary data needs to be trustworthy. If you choose to have someone within your company take the lead on this process, be sure that they are fully on board with the "why diversity and inclusion" concept that your company's leadership team has established.

A diversity survey should be treated as an employee engagement survey, because that's what it is. When a diversity survey is talked about as though it's some separate tool that is going to provide you with magical results, you will inevitably be disappointed. What an employee engagement survey will provide you with is insights into your organizational culture. Your organizational culture is the personality of your company and it's formed by the values and beliefs that are shared by some, most, or all of your employees. Those values and beliefs either create a strong culture or a weak culture. Note that it is not necessarily true that a strong culture is equal to a positive culture.

Getting One-on-One Information through Interviews

Interviews, in conjunction with a survey, can help to identify the places where what is said is not actually practiced. In a culture interview with an employee, when asked what they would tell a friend who wants to interview there, they may say they would tell the friend that if they work hard, there is room for advancement. However, in an anonymous survey, that same question might be answered quite differently. They may say they wouldn't advise a friend to interview there at all or that if they want a chance to advance, they had better get into their supervisor's inner circle.

Conducting interviews as an external consultant allows us to ask questions and gain information that an internal stakeholder would find it difficult to obtain. We work in pairs when possible, to balance our own potential for bias and to provide additional perspectives on what we hear. The anonymous nature of the interviews allows us to dig deeper on circumstances as they arise, correlate frequency of data that occurs across several interviews, and gain clarity and context to conditions that may have been hinted at in survey data.

Interviewees always want to know how they were selected to participate, and we have several factors we use to make the choices. We attempt to get a cross section of employees at different levels of the organization from front line all the way to C-Suite. We include diversity of gender, race, age, and geographic location, as well as function. The questions we ask are customized for each client, but some general questions we ask include:

- With all the competing priorities at your company, where do you personally feel a D&I strategy falls on a scale from 1 to 10?
- What are the values, goals, and norms that drive the behaviors at your company?
- Share an example from an individual/team/company experience that is going exceptionally well in terms of creating a sustainable, diverse, equitable, and inclusive work environment.
- From your perspective, what does "success" look like in terms of a D&I strategy?

Feedback with Group Forums

Group forums are a data-gathering tool that serve additional purposes. Not only do they provide data, but they operate as a communication tool in a time when communication is usually lacking. Group forums can also serve as an indication of action. When employees in your company are clamoring for action to be taken, a group forum can bridge the gap between authentic action and check-the-box activities. For example, many companies have created a DEI council to spearhead diversity initiatives. However, they may not really know what needs to be done. Sitting with that group and really listening to the concerns they raise, as well as hearing what is working, allows them to be heard and begins the process of deciding what needs to be done and in what order. Using a group forum to prioritize activity signals that action will be taken, but that the action will be deliberate and based upon facts and data.

Questions to ask in a group forum can be similar or identical to those asked in an interview, with the understanding that comments may not be as forthcoming since a group discussion can't be anonymous. However, you can impart some confidentiality. Set the tone that the conversation will be candid and that specific comments raised in the group will not be attributed to individuals, but rather to the group as a whole. Keep in mind that the purpose of the forum is to start to gauge consensus of action to be taken and priority of that action.

Taking Up Issues with Town Hall Meetings

Town hall meetings can be used to gather data to get sentiment and know where people stand. Companies can be afraid to announce a town hall meeting because, in their opinion, they have less control over the outcome. They think that if they open the lines of communication, they will have a tough time handling disgruntled comments that they can't or don't want to answer. Allowing that person to have a voice is a good thing. It allows you to identify the potential detractors and you can include them in a one-on-one interview. The detractor feels heard, your employees feel secure that you have a plan for handling concerns when they arise, and you have uncovered concerns that you may otherwise have been unaware of.

Analyzing the Data

Gathering data is only half the battle. The other half is analyzing it. Understanding what the data is telling you is just as important as getting the data to begin with. When conducting surveys in an organization, you have to ensure the questions are answerable and that they correlate to something that can be fixed. The questions need to be tied to behaviors that relate to company values and on the job performance. Asking questions about processes or procedures they would have no knowledge about won't give you any usable data in a survey. Additionally, only asking questions that call for opinion or conjecture isn't helpful either. Therefore, asking men about the use of the mothers' lounge or asking day-shift employees about activities that occur during third shift will provide you with a lot of data that can't be used to uncover or solve any issues that may be occurring in the workplace.

A survey that is attempting to uncover issues of diversity in the workplace should always include demographic questions. You need to know the gender identity, age, geographic office location, race, ethnicity, and whether they have a disability in order to understand what the data is telling you. If we return to my example of the Prudential office where I used to work, a survey would have indicated that we had great diversity numeri-cally, but if questions had been asked about team dynamics, what tools and resources we had to do our job, and the level of support we received from management, you would have seen very differ-ent answers when reviewing the answers of women or of one of the other diversity demographics.

Placement of the demographic questions is important as well. Place them at the front of the survey and you prime the person taking the survey to think more about their differences at work than they otherwise might. Observational selection bias is what happens when we suddenly start noticing things we didn't notice that much before. It happened to me after I purchased a new car; I started seeing that make and model everywhere and I wrongly assumed the number of these types of cars on the road had increased. By placing demographic survey questions at the front of the survey, you inadvertently remind the employee that this survey is about diversity and their subsequent answers can change. Keeping demographic questions at the end also increases response rates and doesn't add to concerns about anonymity.

When analyzing open-ended questions in the survey or feedback received from other data-gathering methods, you can categorize responses in a variety of ways. By planning the questions in advance and categorizing them by relation to the organization versus the team or by areas of review such as belonging, equity, performance, or career, you can begin to see patterns in the qualitative data. It does take more time to line up the information gathered in each category, but this is why working on the data as a team is helpful. The rule of thumb is that when searching for trends in the data, you identify comments that are identical across many employees. A comment from a single employee can be discounted, if minor, but if you identify similar comments from more than three individuals, you have the beginnings of a trend that must be investigated.

Company Culture Can Guide Data

Assessing the culture of your organization will help you to identify the reasons individuals may not adjust to your company culture, which leaves them more likely to be disengaged and less motivated to perform. The strategies used to maintain a strong but less than positive culture include workplace bullying and hostility, which lead to unhappy workers and lawsuits.

According to Ed Schein's model of organizational culture, there are three layers (see Figure 6.1): the artifacts and symbols that are visible, the values and rules of conduct, and the assumed values that are deeper and more difficult to pinpoint.

Before conducting another survey, begin by assessing the visible artifacts. Walk the halls. What is posted on bulletin boards? What is written on whiteboards? How are people dressed? How are they moving through the company? Are they

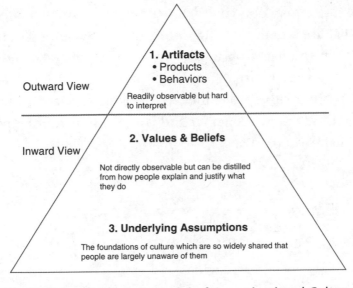

FIGURE 6.1   Ed Schein's Model of Organizational Culture.
Source: Edgar Schein, *Organizational Culture* (1982).

smiling? Walking quickly with little interaction? Is there inter-department movement or does everyone stay confined to their desks? Who eats lunch together?

The less visible values, beliefs, and assumptions will also affect your data. Understanding what those are and how individuals may react to your data-gathering activities will help guide you in choosing the right tool for the workplace. For example, with one particularly conservative client, one of the underlying assumptions in the company was that the conservative view was shared by everyone in the company. Before diving into data gathering, we began with a group forum to gauge what the challenges might be, as well as who our detractors and promoters were. We were able to design a survey that addressed some of the concerns detractors had throughout the company so that the survey would be well-received instead of being seen as intrusive.

As you embark on your data-gathering journey, create questions that are specific to your company, objective in nature, and will obtain the data you need to make the policy changes that your employees desire. Your workforce isn't looking forward to yet another survey, but they are looking forward to positive change. Link the two together and you will find your employees will be happy to participate.

7

Leaders Listen

We have two ears and one mouth for a reason: so that we can listen twice as much as we speak. This concept is attributed to Greek philosopher Epictetus, but regardless of who said it, people have trouble heeding the message and struggle with the concept.

Listening is vital and what should be a relatively simple concept is once again very difficult for companies to put into practice. Take the example of the unconscious bias education you were considering prior to reading this book. In that case, you more than likely made the decision that unconscious bias education was the way to go without conducting an employee survey, without obtaining feedback from your employees, or by extrapolating the opinions of a small group of the loudest voices in your company.

Regardless of how you hear those voices, it's vital that you actually listen to what's being said. By intentionally listening, you gain a greater understanding of the kind of unconscious bias training you need, rather than a cookie-cutter, seemingly one-size-fits-all training that is too broad to be useful. That's why we at Rework Work customize our unconscious bias education to the systematic specifics of your company's needs. With there being over 150 different types of bias, it's vital to identify your needs in order to effectively address them.

Listening Exercise

We'd like to think we are good listeners, but if we ask our partner, children, or even our friends, they would probably tell us otherwise. My company uses a number of tools to aid companies in developing the listening skills of both their employees and their leaders, but our go-to resource is an exercise that when practiced in pairs, results in immediate takeaways that an employee can apply to their role. This activity exemplifies what listening should look like. It is a powerful exercise that allows individuals not only to listen, but to finally experience what it feels like to be truly listened to and to be heard.

After dividing the participants into pairs, we provide them with a question or prompt they will respond to and give them 15–20 minutes for the activity. No matter how many times we conduct this activity, the results continue to surprise me. Participants leave having built trust with their partner, have a newfound sense of connectedness, and a heightened, positive emotional state. In some cases, it is the first time an employee has truly felt heard at work and it is an overwhelming experience, one they didn't know they were missing.

Why does listening work? What we have observed when conducting the sessions with the general employee population base is that the benefits exceed our expectations. The feedback we receive is that the senior leaders should be conducting the exact same exercise, that it should be mandatory for all managers and supervisors, and that they wish they had more time to participate in the activity because they find it to be extremely beneficial. They use the time to increase the connectedness of their peers and to create trust among their colleagues and they find themselves unexpectedly excited to return to their work and put what they have learned into practice.

Improve Employee Engagement

The Society for Human Resource Management (SHRM) reported in a publication, "Employees who feel listened to feel more connected with the employer and in turn feel more engaged and motivated to do the best work for the organization." The same publication also cites a poll conducted by John Izzo, author of *Stepping Up: How Taking Responsibility Changes Everything*. In that poll of 675 professional workers in the United States and Canada, he found that 64% of respondents agreed that "leaders making decisions without seeking input" was their biggest problem.

Employees who feel heard are more engaged and motivated and the statistics around employee engagement and motivation cannot be ignored. According to Deloitte University's Leadership Center for Inclusion, 83% of millennials are more likely to be actively engaged if they believe their company creates a diverse and inclusive culture and, according to Gallup, only three out of ten employees feel heard at work. However, when you improve that number from three to six, companies see a 27% reduction in turnover, a 40% reduction in safety incidents, and a 12% increase in productivity.[1]

Listen to Let Ideas Soar

Leaders listen, not only for the potential to hear great ideas, but also for the ability to step in and prevent great ideas from being stifled before they have had the chance to be expressed.

Microaggressions

By now you have probably heard the term "microaggression," but not very many people really know what it is, and if you have, it has become polarizing. Much like "white privilege" or "anti-racist," the term elicits an immediate response in people, especially those who don't understand the meaning, so I think it's important to spend a little time defining terms and concepts.

The term "microaggression" has been around since the 1970s but it was finally defined by Harvard psychiatrist Chester Pierce. Initially it was a way to explain verbal and nonverbal indignities, mainly toward African Americans, but today that has been expanded upon by modern psychologists.

It is not a concept focused solely on race, but it has roots in its effect on African Americans because of the prevalence and because of just how deep racism runs. The concept has now been expanded to other marginalized groups and addresses usual comments or behaviors, environmental slights or snubs, and traits

[1]https://www2.deloitte.com/content/dam/Deloitte/us/Documents/about-deloitte/us-inclus-millennial-influence-120215.pdf; Jake Herway, "How to Create a Culture of Psychological Safety," Gallup, December 7, 2017, https://www.gallup.com/workplace/236198/create-culture-psychological-safety.aspx.

about a demographic that communicate a stereotypically derogatory or negative message, impacting not only Black people but Asian people, older people, women in general across all races, the LGBTQ community, people in lower socioeconomic groups, and of course people with disabilities.

It is an occurrence that is apparent across all classes and genders and races because of the way in which we can use words to hurt people. A microaggression is a comment or behavior that is based on a stereotype or bias about a demographic. Dr. Derald Wing Sue, a psychology professor at Columbia University, uses "microaggressions" as an umbrella term to define three subterms: microassaults, microinsults, and microinvalidations:

- **Microassault:** A microassault is intentional; it is hurtful and direct. Saying "You don't act like a normal Asian girl" is an example of a microassault.
- **Microinsult:** A microinsult is usually unintentional, but it is usually based in a biased belief. Assuming a Black student is on a football scholarship is an example of a microinsult.
- **Microinvalidation:** A microinvalidation disregards the feelings and experiences of the receiver.

Reducing the occurrence of all three subcategories of microaggressions begins with awareness. If you witness a microaggression, speak up; don't stay silent. Acting as an ally in that moment includes listening to and hearing how you can support the person.

Microinequities

Not to confuse the issue, but there are also microinequities. In a paper titled "Micro-Affirmations and Micro-Inequities," Mary Rowe describes ways in which individuals are singled out,

ignored, and overlooked.[2] Others taking credit for your ideas or
your work, being told you speak English very well, and hearing
someone say they don't see color because we are all just human
are all microinequities.

Respond to Micromessages

With that being said, nobody cares if you understand the definition of a microaggression or microinequity. But what people do
care about is how you treat them. They care that you listen, they
care that you pay attention to the cues that are apparent and
that you step up or step in to help. They care if you ask questions when you don't understand and apologize when you make a
mistake. They care that you authentically listen and don't ignore
their concerns.

There are ways that you as a leader can not only learn to
respond to these micromessages, but can also help your team do
this as well:

- **Process.** Process what you're feeling, even if that means
  you just have to stop and take a breath. We are all so concerned with silence in a conversation that we rush to fill in
  the spaces. It's okay to wait a beat or two before speaking.

- **Ask.** Ask if you heard correctly. Repeat what you thought
  you heard and clarify before responding.

- **Understand.** Seek to understand what they are trying to
  convey. What was their motivation? Did they have positive intent?

---

[2]https://www.researchgate.net/publication/265450386_Micro-affirmations_Micro-
inequities.

- **Share.** Share how this impacts you and your perspective on the comment. Let them see another point of view.

- **Explore.** Explore ways to reframe the statement so they won't repeat the mistake.

Difficult conversations don't have to be difficult and you don't have to be confrontational to confront bias at work. Employees are looking to their managers and to the senior leaders in their company for direction on how to address these topics. They want to feel that their company hears them when they say it's time to act and they want to be secure in the knowledge they know what to do. You can't boil the ocean, but you should choose one activity that you can implement as part of your action plan to address unconscious bias at work.

Action

8

Leaders Take Action

Now that your leadership team is aligned in its purpose and valuation of increased diversity and inclusion, it is time to get to work. So often organizations want to jump right to this step to check the box and move on, and I hope that by now you understand that D&I initiatives can only move forward successfully and sustainably when there is genuine buy-in based on real information from your employees.

Ultimately, the goal of diversity and inclusion is to establish equity across your entire organization, but equity doesn't happen by just talking about it.

Equity is literally the quality of being fair and impartial. Equity at work requires the fair treatment, access, opportunity, and advancement for all people, while also working to identify and eliminate barriers that have prevented the full participation of some employees. Yet the word "fair" can be problematic.

Life is not fair. You play with the hand you're dealt, and you don't complain. However, a workplace is a forum that is created by the leaders. There isn't chance at play. The practices, policies, and procedures have been put in place by people just like you. And in the same way they were deliberately created, they can be amended to address the barriers that also exist, whether intentional or not. But it's the "addressing barriers" part that people struggle with. It can give the impression you may be required to give people special treatment in order to right a past wrong.

Life may not be fair, but does that make it right? We blindly accept these sayings as though once it's been uttered, we've made a binding covenant, it's set in stone and never to be reviewed again. You may wonder about whether you have the power to take action and do something about inequities in society, but you definitely have the ability to take action to do something about workplace inequities.

There is also some confusion about the difference between equity and equality. Figure 8.1 provides a visual that clears this up. Equality is about making everyone equal. Equality sounds as though it is fair, but the visual demonstrates that when you have a barrier

Equality:

The assumption is that everyone benefits from the same supports. This is equal treatment.

Equity:

Everyone gets the support they need (this is the concept of "affirmative action"), thus producing equity.

FIGURE 8.1 Equality versus Equity.

in place, equality is not enough. Equity is actually what is needed. The barrier is what makes equity necessary, rather than equality.

Affirmative Action

Affirmative action is probably the most misunderstood term when discussing diversity and inclusion in America. Affirmative action at its base level is exactly what the two words mean from a literal sense.

The word "affirmative" literally means consenting to or agreeing with a statement, while "action" literally means the fact or process of doing something. Therefore, affirmative action in its literal sense means agreeing to do something. That's it. I enjoy oversimplifying things to make it easy for us to remember, and in this case, it works very well.

If you can remember that affirmative action means agreeing to do something, then you are halfway to understanding the concept and its application.

The other half is the application. Affirmative action is a federal initiative that is a response to the Civil Rights Act of 1964. It is a way for universities and the federal government to attempt to counter the racist policies that were in place for hundreds of years.

Since it is a federal policy, there is no state application unless your state has specific equal opportunity laws. The guidelines around an official affirmative action policy couldn't be less specific if they tried, which is why I focus on the literal definition of affirmative action. If a company, a university, a federal contractor, a small business, or anyone who wants to hire an individual makes the decision to put a policy in place that could possibly increase the representation of traditionally underrepresented groups of individuals in the hiring process, then it is for all intents and purposes an affirmative action program. Therefore, if a company decides they will visit an HBCU (Historically Black College or University) in order to increase the number of diverse applicants to their hiring pool, then it can be considered an example of an affirmative action policy.

Equity at Work

Using the 2020 global pandemic as an example, when COVID-19 resulted in governments shutting down entire cities and companies having no choice but to allow their employees to work from home, many employers struggled with how to offer accommodations to those who needed it. Should they start meetings later in the day so that parents could attend to homeschooling children in the morning? But what about individuals who don't have children? Then when restrictions were eased and guidelines were provided for conducting business, employers wondered whether they should make everyone work from home. But what about those employees who did not have a good internet connection at home and would have preferred to work in the office? Could they allow it? Should they allow it? Wouldn't it seem unfair that some individuals were going into the office while others were working from home?

The answer to all those questions is common sense and communication. There is no one-size-fits-all solution. Sometimes equality isn't what is needed. Talking to your employees and asking them what they need to get the job done can provide you with a win-win solution that works for both parties and those solutions will look different for different employees. It is not necessary to treat people equally in order to be equitable.

Continuing with the 2020 global pandemic as an example, employees expected their employers to provide solutions. Action was demanded and some leaders stepped up, as in the case of

Aon, a global insurance and consulting firm. CEO Greg Case gave up 50% of his salary for the remainder of 2020, beginning in April 2020, and cut pay for 70% of employees above an undisclosed ceiling, in order to ensure no one at Aon would lose their job. He then restored their pay less than 60 days later, once the dire projections they were operating under were not as stark as feared. He also provided a bonus of 5% to "recognize their personal resilience and dedication." The salaries of executive officers and board members were not restored from the 50% pay cut.[1]

Meanwhile, other leaders left employees feeling let down. In March 2020, MGM Resorts International furloughed and laid off thousands of workers, yet somehow managed to pay $32 million to their CEO, who voluntarily resigned and should have received nothing, according to his original contract with the company. At a time when communities were relying on their local grocery store to stock up and keep stores open, Kroger stopped providing hazard pay of an additional $2 per hour for essential workers. Company leaders acknowledge sales are at higher levels while employees were working "around the clock," but they have not announced pay cuts for top executives who are not on the front lines in their stores. The individuals who *are* on the front lines are employees of lower socioeconomic status who can't afford to quit. These actions are indicative of a company's priorities and the value they place on their employees. As of September 2020, the United Food and Commercial Workers Union was still fighting to have Kroger provide hazard pay in a time when the grocery chain has reported a 14 percent increase in earnings.

Looking outside of the pandemic, the tech company Salesforce has received a lot of praise, and rightfully so, regarding the

---

[1]https://www.chicagotribune.com/coronavirus/ct-coronavirus-chicago-aon-restore-salary-20200630-5ocmwtsgmbhyfmtbh4gxdiwff4-story.html.

leadership decision to address their pay discrepancies. In 2015, CEO Marc Benioff said, "I simply did not believe that pay disparities could be pervasive. 'Impossible,' I told them. 'That's not right. That's not how we operate.'" After conducting an audit of the 17,000 employees they had at the time and finding that "glaring differences were scattered throughout every division, department, and geographical region," they didn't give everyone a 5% raise across the board – that would only have perpetuated the gap. In this instance, they had to treat everyone equitably in order to get to equality.

Leadership Development

An equitable leader takes action but does so with an understanding of what the barriers are in place for certain segments of the employee population. When I begin working with an organization to address their diversity and inclusion concerns and implement a strategy, I find that many of the issues with managers and leaders are due to a lack of adequate development. When you find a manager who isn't performing well or who doesn't mesh well with the team, it might be immediately assumed it's related to a dimension of diversity, rather than attribute it to poor management training or a lack of leadership development.

Going Beyond What's on Paper

On June 15, 2020, the U.S. Supreme Court ruled that under the Civil Rights Act of 1964, employees cannot be fired because they are gay or transgender. Within 24 hours of the ruling, human resource departments across the country made quick work of updating legal posters, employee handbooks, and any other publication that references their company's policies and procedures. On paper, these companies look like they've covered the bases of compliance, but unless time is taken to inform the leadership team of the changes and their long-term effects, new policies fail to be implemented. This is where leadership development is so important.

Do your hiring managers understand they can no longer make decisions that may discriminate against someone simply because they are gay or transgender, such as firing or refusing to hire? Do you have procedures in place to ensure they know how to comply and are they aware that compliance is the minimum expectation, not the ceiling?

This work of diversity and inclusion is challenging, but it's only made more difficult because companies have neglected their responsibility to develop other leaders in their organization. Without continuous professional development, attempts at building diversity and inclusion are like building a house on a crumbling foundation – destined for collapse.

Making Development Ongoing

Professional development should be ongoing. That development should come in the form of hands-on, experiential learning that allows individuals to practice what they are learning. Have you ever attended a webinar and thought about all the great points while it was happening, walked away thinking you're going to implement a few of the things you learned, and by the following day forgot all about it and continued with business as usual? We all have. That's what happens when you implement training that doesn't allow leaders the opportunity to develop real-world answers to actual challenges in their workplace, and it's worse if you can't remember the last time your management team has been offered internal development.

Professional industry development is great, but making change stick will require you to offer development that affords your managers time to bond as a team and learn the internal practices and procedures that have changed. You may not have a large learning and development team or you may not have one at all. Get creative. Encourage managers to offer their own form of training once per month or once per quarter. Send them for external professional development and task them with coming back and facilitating a session for their peers on the applicability of that development to their workplace.

We tend to be so task-oriented that we forget to check in with our budding leaders. Although it seems to be such a small thing, regularly touching base with your leadership team builds trust and keeps communication open, creating a space for better flow-down and accountability for procedural changes.

Establish Employee Resource Groups as a Resource to the Business

Employee Resource Groups (ERGs) or Business Resource Groups (BRGs) began their existence as affinity groups. They were simply a way for individuals in underrepresented groups to connect and have a safe space where they would feel included.

I'd like to say that supporting the formation of Employee Resource Groups is no longer necessary as a safe space, but in some companies that haven't started any of the work we've discussed thus far, that wouldn't be true. More progressive companies have evolved their ERGs to harness their diversity as a benefit to the company. While those who don't understand them can see them as divisive, ERGs actually provide a signal to those who have formally been excluded that they are welcome. ERGs also provide a communication channel that allows you to answer the question "Is your workplace inclusive?" as well as provide a business resource for maintaining diversity and inclusion in the workplace.

Nielsen collects data that is trusted and used by their clients to make important decisions. Matthew Hanzlik, director of Diversity and Inclusion at Nielsen, worked with me to present their ERG data to a large group of diversity professionals at a conference. From their example, you can see just how far-reaching the impact is of their Employee Resource Groups. Nielsen has more than 5,000 members of nine ERGs and engages more than 13,000 employees across groups in 77 countries. They demonstrate how you can harness the diversity of your employees, engage them in business initiatives, assist in your diversity and inclusion strategy by being a sounding board prior to implementation, help with retention of underrepresented groups of employees within your company, provide a perspective that can be overlooked in your marketing efforts, and act as a large source of candidate referrals. As an example of the types of groups your company can support, take a look at Nielsen's ERGs (as of March 2019) that demonstrate that diversity isn't all about race, ethnicity, and gender:

- HOLA – Hispanic Organizations of Leaders in Action
- SABLE – Sustaining Active Black Leadership & Empowerment
- PRIDE – Lesbian, Gay, Bisexual, Transgender & Allies
- AAL – Asian Affinity Link
- ADEPT – Abled & Disabled Employees Partnering Together
- WIN – Women in Nielsen
- SERV – Support & Employee Resources for Veterans
- N-GEN – Nielsen Generation
- MOSAIC – Multinational Organization Supporting An Inclusive Culture

An additional example is that of the CEO of a large entertainment company in Los Angeles. His Chief Diversity Officer worked with a group of employees who supported the creation of ERGs, but the CEO was less than receptive to the idea. He was stingy with his support, both in time and in funds. However, he gave it enough lip service to allow her to move forward. He signed the formation paperwork and approved a small seed fund, but it wasn't until he attended one of their meetings and saw the impact it had on the employees that he truly understood its value. Then he became a true advocate. He witnessed equity in action and it completely changed his attitude toward ERGs.

Creation of a D&I Council

I'm looking for a place where I can feel supported.

I hear that statement so often from people from all walks of life and at varying levels of their career. We want to belong. So it's heartbreaking to hear the stories of people who don't feel they belong while at work.

A few years ago, I met a woman who works in the HR department of her company. It's her job to help the 7,000 employees in her company, yet every day, she comes to work and does not feel supported. Every day, she feels alone. She told me that she felt isolated and alone while at work, so much so that as she talked to me about it, she had to fight back tears.

Do you recognize this woman? Is she you, or is she an employee in your company?

When organizations don't have enough employees of a particular group to warrant creating an ERG, an Inclusion Council can be a substitute. Another great purpose of an Inclusion Council is as a governing body for the various Employee Resource Groups that may be available in your company. This allows for sharing of resources, the discussion of an upcoming holiday celebration, a cohesive plan for events for the calendar year, and transparency and collaboration across all groups.

The Inclusion or DEI Council can also be the spokespersons who work with the senior leadership team on the D&I strategy for the organization.

Equity Tools That Work

Utilizing ERGs and a D&I Council work to ensure there is oversight, that a review or analysis of policies happens, and gives a voice to those who want to be a champion for diversity and inclusion. It starts with culture change, and the people who can help speed up that change can be found within ERGs, in your leadership teams, and in your Inclusion Councils.

Promoting diversity within the organization happens as the culture begins to change and that change gets spearheaded by individuals who keep equity at the forefront. When done right, they promote employee engagement, connect to the communities where the employees work, and increase the bottom line of the company by expanding their marketing power.

The divide felt within your company will melt away when diverse individuals are accepted, different cultures are acknowledged, and everyone respects the unique skills and experiences brought into the company. But it's never that easy. Sometimes you have to force individuals to see what (or who) has been right in front of them all along.

The Rooney Rule is one tool that emerged from the NFL's lopsided hiring practices and has since sparked similar rules in other industries, such as the Mansfield Rule in the legal field. The Rooney Rule was implemented in 2003 and requires NFL teams to interview at least one candidate of color for a head coach position.

Assembly Bill No. 979

On September 30, 2020, Governor Gavin Newsom signed Assembly Bill No. 979, which requires California corporations that are publicly held and headquartered in California to ensure their board of directors includes at least one director from an underrepresented community by December 31, 2021.

AB 979 defines "underrepresented community" as "self-identification as Black, African American, Hispanic, Latino, Asian, Pacific Islander, Native American, Native Hawaiian, Alaska Native, gay, lesbian, bisexual, or transgender."

By the close of the following year (December 31, 2022), corporations with a board size of nine or more directors must have a minimum of three directors from underrepresented communities on their boards, and corporations with a board size of more than four but fewer than nine directors must have a minimum of two directors from underrepresented communities.

Starting no later than March 1, 2022, the California Secretary of State will publish annual reports on its website documenting compliance with these requirements. Companies that fail to timely comply will be fined $100,000 for the first violation and $300,000 for subsequent violations.

This bill is similar to Senate Bill 826, signed into law in 2018, which required publicly held corporations headquartered in California to include women on their boards.

The rule was expanded in 2009 to include general manager jobs and other similar front-office positions. When nearly 68% of the NFL's players are African American, it is deplorable that African

Americans aren't equally or equitably represented in the numbers for professional positions, team presidents, or head coach positions.

For the Rooney Rule to be effective, it requires there be a meaningful interview of a person of color, not a token interview for the sake of optics. It also requires this rule to apply to the assistant coach/coordinator position because it is logical that a candidate with coordinator experience will be a more viable candidate than one without. Prior to 2020, the Rooney Rule did nothing to address that pipeline issue even though a proposal was put forth in 2013 to do that (it was rejected). The NFL has corrected their misstep and as of May 2020, they require teams to interview at least two external minority candidates for head coaching openings and at least one minority candidate for any coordinator job.

Promoting equity gets candidates in the room who have been traditionally overlooked due to bias, habit, ignorance, and tight networks that haven't let outsiders in. This rule doesn't guarantee a job for a candidate of color; it simply allows them to be considered to enter the room when the door was previously closed to them; much like California Assembly Bill 979 has been put in place to give women a seat at the table. When the Rooney Rule was first implemented there was a lot of backlash and insinuation that a head coach who was considered as a result of the rule wouldn't have credibility as a coach. I think Hall of Famer Tony Dungy would disagree.

Xerox, Facebook, Intel, Pinterest, and even Amazon have created their own version of the rule, while the Pentagon evaluated its viability in its efforts to diversify officer corps. It's time for leaders who now have a greater understanding of equity as a concept to take action to draft an effective policy, as well as a plan for measuring effectiveness.

9

Inclusion Is Intentional

We've all done it. We've asked a woman when her baby is due because she was a little heavier than when we last saw her, but she wasn't actually pregnant. We have asked how their son is doing because the child's hair is short, but that child is actually female. We view the world through our own perspectives without regard for how someone else may be experiencing things. We're taught to follow the golden rule of treating others how we would want to be treated. However, in the workplace as in life, we begin to learn that we should have been taught the platinum rule: treat others how they would like to be treated, rather than how we assume they want to be treated.

Accenture discovered that not everyone at their company felt included when they started the "Inclusion Starts with I" campaign. Ellyn Shook, Accenture's chief leadership and human resources officer, wanted to answer the question "Did our people really feel like they belong?" They decided to create an internal video that profoundly explored the question of inclusiveness. In the video, Accenture employees hold up signs with an experience of bias and as the video continues, employees hold up new messages that explain how each individual has the power to make others feel included.

Inclusion most definitely starts with "I" because it is very difficult to be inclusive when you are not open: open to new people, open to new ideas, open to different perspectives and new possibilities.

Being Open to New Possibilities

In my course on diversity recruiting, I discuss that when recruiters are screening candidates, after they've identified a potential candidate based on their resume but before they invite the candidate to a formal interview, they should stop themselves from rejecting a potentially great candidate because of a bias, and start the screening process by focusing in on the attributes that are required for the job. By maintaining the qualifications as the only criteria for rejection, there is less likelihood they will inadvertently eliminate someone because of a bias. When screening to include, rather than exclude, not only will the candidate pool be more diverse, but inclusion for the candidates overall will increase. If you've ever had quite a few diverse candidates in the candidate pool but none of them made it to the interview stage, this is why.

Practice Openness

Do you try new foods? Listen to different music? Have you learned another language? Do you travel outside the country?

If inclusion starts with "I," these activities will help you listen to and be open to ideas from others. Using connection requests on LinkedIn as an example, what's your personal acceptance policy? Do you only accept requests from people you know? I thought this sounded strange but was surprised to find that a number of individuals act from this philosophy. Which leads me to ask, "Why are you on LinkedIn?" If you only accept requests from people you know, are you simply using LinkedIn as a personal rolodex? And if so, does your personal philosophy change when you need to be connected to someone outside of your network? Do you then expect someone who has a much more open philosophy to connect you to someone you need to know and, if so, do you recognize the hypocrisy?

Inclusion Counts If You're Included

As open as I can be, I also recognize the benefits of joining a private club. I was invited to become a member of a club that requires a rather large initiation fee to join, as well as payment of monthly dues. There's a lot of socializing and networking happening in this club. Many of the members are businesspeople who use the club to obtain sales leads and close business deals.

There isn't anything wrong with being a member of a private club, but what *is* wrong is denying that members have privileges and advantages that are not accessible to others. Someone who would not have been invited to – let alone been able to afford to – become a member of a private club is at a disadvantage.

We tend to believe the best of ourselves and the worst of others. We assume we have achieved everything we have because we worked so hard, much harder than everyone else. But did we really? Sometimes what we achieved has been partly due to circumstance.

It's easier and more fulfilling to believe we worked hard and achieved than to believe that someone else worked just as hard, or perhaps even harder, and was still denied an opportunity. It doesn't make sense to us so we rationalize. And when we haven't felt it because it hasn't affected us, it is extremely difficult to digest.

Connections Matter: Not Everyone Is the Same and That's Okay

Inclusion requires us to consider other perspectives, to open our eyes to the plight of others and demonstrate empathy. We look at our own success in a positive light while downplaying the achievements of others. Have you ever thought that other people aren't doing as well because they aren't trying hard enough or working hard enough? Or have you acknowledged the good fortune that has crossed your own path prior to making a comparison? It's this perspective that can make it difficult to be inclusive because we believe the other person isn't deserving.

You've probably heard the expression about trying to fit a square peg into a round hole. Think about our connection request philosophy on LinkedIn in relation to this idea. Society is the round hole and the square pegs are those people we exclude. If you find yourself asking the square pegs why they just can't seem to make it work and fit in as you have, it might be time to acknowledge they're not square pegs at all. You have simply perceived them that way and they could fit in if you let them.

The success of LinkedIn when we are open is supported by sociologist and Stanford professor Mark S. Granovetter. He published a paper titled "The Strength of Weak Ties" and a book titled *Getting a Job: A Study of Contacts and Careers* and persuasively demonstrates that weak-tie networking is far superior to strong-tie networking. A weak tie is easier to maintain, as on a social network. A weak tie could be a second- or third-degree connection, but it could also be a first connection who is simply an acquaintance or someone you don't know very well.

When working to improve the diversity of our own networks, we have to be more open and utilize weak ties. In 2019, when LinkedIn CEO Jeff Weiner stepped down to focus on "advancing diversity, inclusion, and belonging at LinkedIn through continuing work on innovative recruiting practices, allyship and mentoring efforts, unconscious bias education, apprenticeship programs for people with non-traditional backgrounds, and ongoing ERG support," one of the things he admitted they needed to do was pay attention to the unintended consequences that may be caused by the LinkedIn platform.

He asks, "What happens if you have the aptitude, what if you have the skills, what if you have the grit, resilience, and growth mind-set, what if you're exactly the person our organizations are looking to hire? What if you're a star talent but you didn't grow up in a high-income neighborhood, didn't go to a top school, and you haven't worked for a top company?" What happens is some of you will never meet that person because your personal philosophy is to network only with people you already know.

Inclusion Can Be Learned

Inclusion is an intentional act, so consider a show called *Through the Wormhole*, hosted by Morgan Freeman. In the episode "Are We All Bigots?" a scientist demonstrated how we can actively include by using different strains of mice. Let's label them Strain A and Strain B.

Two mice were put into an area where part of the space was caged. There was a mechanism that the mice had been trained to use; when pressed, it would allow the trapped mouse out of the caged area. When two mice from Strain A were in the experiment, one would use the mechanism to let the other out of the cage. The same was true for the mice from Strain B. However, when a mouse from Strain A was put into the experimental area with a mouse from Strain B, they would not let each other out. They would bypass the mechanism and leave the other caged in.

The scientist then took mice from both Strain A and Strain B and socialized them together. At the end of their shared time together, she put a mouse from Strain A into the experimental area with a mouse from Strain B – one it hadn't been socialized with. The mouse from Strain A used the mechanism and let the new mouse from Strain B out of the cage. By socializing the mice, their behavior changed. They learned to include other mice they had previously excluded.

This shows that there is hope for us. We can learn inclusion. The culture of your organization, your quality of life, and your success as a leader is affected by your ability to socialize with others who are different than you, both in and out of work.

Actively Work Towards Inclusion

It's as simple as having lunch with someone different or asking someone new to work with you on a project. Spend a little time learning about views that differ from yours. If you can accept that we are all different, and agree to respect those differences rather than simply tolerate them, inclusion, rather than exclusion, will be your default.

What does your network look like? Is your personal and professional network homogenous? Do the people in your inner circle have the same religious beliefs? Are they all in the same socioeconomic class? Do they all look like you? Make a concerted effort to expand your network by including new people in your circle. Take deliberate steps to introduce yourself to individuals who are outside of your network, who are a different race, gender, socioeconomic status, or from a vastly different geographic region. The next time someone asks why your recruiting pipeline is devoid of a specific demographic, rather than say you don't know, take action to identify two or three individuals so that the next time, you can provide referrals rather than acceptance of the status quo.

Pepsi Falls Short with Ad

The business application can be demonstrated in what has been called the "worst ad ever," created by Pepsi in 2017. As described by *Teen Vogue*:[1]

In the commercial, we see a blonde, bewigged Kendall [Jenner] in the midst of a photo shoot, while a protest takes place on the streets just steps away from where she is posing. As "Lions" by Skip Marley plays in the background, the camera cuts between the protesters, many of whom are artists. It's an inclusive crowd for sure, with people of all identities joining together to march with signs depicting the peace symbol.

As the ad continues, it becomes increasingly obvious that Kendall wants to join the marchers, and she even locks eyes with one of the protesters who nods at her as if to say, "Come on." In the ad's climactic moments, Kendall removes her blonde wig, wipes the dark lipstick from her mouth, and filters into the crowd. She is seen approaching a line of police officers, and she hands one an ice-cold can of Pepsi. There is a pause, and then the officer pops open the can, yielding cheers and applause from the protesters. The words "live bolder, live louder, live for now," fill the screen as the ad comes to an end.

If you never actually saw the ad, you may want to read the *Teen Vogue* article because they did a fantastic job of explaining

---

[1]https://www.teenvogue.com/story/pepsi-commercial-kendall-jenner-reaction.

why the ad is tone deaf, exploitive, and insensitive. Late night TV host Jimmy Kimmel said out loud what nearly everyone was thinking: "The fact that this somehow made it through – I can't imagine how many meetings, and edits, and pitches, and then got the thumbs-up from who knows how many people is absolutely mind-boggling," he said.

What every person of color was thinking, and correctly it appears, is that there couldn't have been a person of color with any authority anywhere near this project or the ad wouldn't have seen the light of day. There are six key people who are credited with creating the ad and, of course, all six are white. Inclusion could have prevented Pepsi from issuing the standard apology: "Pepsi was trying to project a global message of unity, peace and understanding. Clearly, we missed the mark, and we apologize. We did not intend to make light of any serious issue."

Tokenism and Inclusion

Tokenism can be the downfall of inclusivity. As defined by Oxford Languages, tokenism is the practice of making only a perfunctory or symbolic effort to do a particular thing, especially by recruiting a small number of people from underrepresented groups in order to give the appearance of sexual or racial equality within a workforce.

If the creative team at Pepsi had included individuals of color, could this debacle have been avoided? I'd like to think the answer is yes. More nuanced is, if they had included more than one individual of color, would they have had the psychological safety needed to speak up and be heard in the meeting? Unfortunately, the answer there is probably no and if that's the case, it would be attributed to tokenism.

Examples of tokenism can be a lone woman in an office dominated by men or a Black person being offered the job of Chief Diversity Officer primarily or entirely to make an organization look fair. When you practice tokenism you harm the person, the company, and the overall field of diversity and inclusion because it is inauthentic. In a company where we conducted a gender audit, gender in senior leadership was a big issue because all of the women would leave right before they had the opportunity to be promoted or within the first year of being promoted. One example was a woman who was promoted to the executive table but was not afforded the responsibility of having actual direct reports. She was given an advanced title in name only, but with no real authority. Unsurprisingly, she left the organization.

10

Belonging
Makes an Impact

Have you ever been visiting a friend whose family spoke a language you didn't understand? Or maybe you misunderstood a wedding invitation and showed up in formal attire while everyone else was very casual. Perhaps it was as simple as being underdressed at a business event. Regardless of the circumstance, the reaction is the same. You feel out of place. In the examples of attire, your thoughts wander from deciding whether to leave to whether anyone really noticed.

In these examples of feeling out of place, the difference is that you can leave, or you can change clothes. The feeling doesn't last, and you're not left with the sense that something about you, which you cannot change, is flawed or wrong. This feeling of being an outsider makes an impact. But it's the exact opposite impact you want to make as a leader.

I spent much of my life wanting to belong, attempting to fit in and failing miserably at it.

- I was a Black girl in every all-white school I attended in London. If I could count on one hand the number of Black children in the school (the entire school), that would have been a lot.
- I was an intelligent girl who read faster than everyone in class, completed her math problems before everyone in class, and so frustrated one of my teachers with my intelligence that he ripped a book I was reading out of my hands and threw it in the trash.
- I was the only Black girl on my block with no friends after my only friend was told by his mom that he couldn't play with me anymore because I was Black.
- I was a Black girl with a British accent in all Black and Latino schools in Brooklyn, New York.
- I was a Black girl in Brooklyn during the rise of rap and R&B who didn't know the music or the slang or the dance moves. I was the same race, but I wasn't the same ethnicity.

It is only now, in my work as a diversity leader, that I see the strength in my inability to belong anywhere. It makes me empathetic. It allows me to see perspectives of others and it makes it just a little easier for me to explain concepts like this to you.

Belonging Is Vital to Performance and Well-Being

We all want to belong. In fact, we have a primal need to feel that way. In 1943, psychologist Abraham Maslow first introduced his now-famous hierarchy of needs theory in the *Psychological Review* (see Figure 10.1), a science journal published by Princeton University. In "A Theory of Human Motivation," Maslow wrote that humans are more motivated to meet basic or deficiency needs, before they work to satisfy more advanced needs.

Maslow argued that belonging is a deficiency need, meaning that the longer that need goes unmet, the stronger the urge becomes to meet it. Hunger, for example, is also a deficiency need – the longer you go without eating, the hungrier you get. Ultimately, he writes, individuals aren't motivated to meet the esteem and self-actualization needs unless the psychological and physiological needs are met first. The short of it is, people are

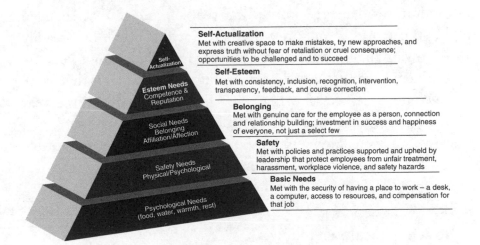

FIGURE 10.1 Maslow's Hierarchy of Needs Theory.
Source: Based on Maslow, A. H. (1943). "A theory of human motivation." *Psychological Review*, 50(4), 370–396. doi:10.1037/h0054346

unable to reach their full potential if they don't feel as though they belong.

Belonging is fundamental to our sense of happiness and well-being. Isolation, loneliness, and low social status can harm a person's subjective sense of well-being, as well as his or her intellectual achievement, immune function, and health. Research by social psychologist and Stanford assistant professor Gregory Walton shows that even a single instance of exclusion can undermine well-being, IQ test performance, and self-control. Creating a sense of belonging had a particularly dramatic effect on students' achievement in Walton's paper "A Brief Social-Belonging Intervention Improves Academic and Health Outcomes of Minority Students." The minority achievement gap is a form of self-doubt and imposter syndrome suffered by minority students and women in overwhelmingly male-dominated majors and manifests itself as a disparity in academic performance.

In this particular study involving African American and white college freshmen in a predominantly white university, an intervention was delivered in the first year of college that changed the trajectory of minority students' achievement by steadily improving their grades all the way through their senior year. By intervening and actively demonstrating to the students they were welcome, accepted, and that they belong, over the three-year observation period the African American students who took part in the study had higher grade-point averages relative to multiple control groups, and the minority achievement gap overall was reduced by 50% – an overwhelming increase.

How to Educate Employees

Education of the concept of belonging is a necessary part of ensuring the successful implementation of a diversity and inclusion strategy within your company. Unconscious bias education is necessary to fully understand the concept of belonging. Knowing how important belonging is to the health and welfare of your employees, it's easier to understand when to begin education.

A big complaint or excuse we hear for not implementing unconscious bias education in the workplace is that it doesn't work. Conduct an internet search to determine if unconscious bias training works and you will find thousands of articles telling you no.

What those articles fail to express is the idea that unconscious bias training may not work because companies are substituting unconscious bias training for leadership development, management training, role-specific education such as recruitment practices, human resource expertise, cultural competence, or even global enterprise management experience.

What I find myself offering in place of, or in addition to, unconscious bias education, is conflict management, how to have difficult conversations, how to create trust and psychological safety at work, and how to be an ally.

Putting Bias Education into Motion

In the case of belonging, and the impact it makes in a workplace, the link between unconscious bias education and belonging becomes clearer. I previously defined unconscious bias as a way for us to quickly categorize other people without thinking and as a shortcut our brains take, which is affected by social, cultural, and religious norms.

In an education session, employees want to know how this definition of unconscious bias relates to their particular job. They need to know how to identify it when they see it, how to tackle it when it comes up, and how to address it if they are the victim of it. This is why offering unconscious bias training before you have taken the time to know your data can sometimes seem to cause more problems than existed previously.

The perception may be that you didn't have any workplace challenges until you offered unconscious bias education. But the reality is that the problems were always there and simply offering unconscious bias education without identifying and acknowledging the underlying challenges merely heightens the frustration of the individuals who already knew these challenges existed.

But when you offer unconscious bias education, prior to committing not only to uncovering the challenges but also to offering solutions, you increase the distrust in the company because you have not offered your employees an avenue to manage or address their concerns. You also have not indicated to your employees that you are interested in learning what those challenges might be or that you are willing to allocate the resources necessary to address them.

An Example of Not Having All the Facts

Offering unconscious bias education prior to knowing your data also causes you to solve for problems that may not exist. Take the example of a client who requested coaching for one of their managers. The manager in question was universally disliked by her direct reports. The company wanted to offer her development opportunities as a first step and thought coaching would help.

The company thought the manager might be racist and if that was the case, they would have to fire her. But they wanted to have their bases covered before they took that step. Why did they think she may be racist? All of her direct reports were Black and/or Latino and the manager was white, and they were consistently complaining about her behavior toward them. She was condescending and made it clear she thought her staff were beneath her.

After being coached, the report that was prepared for the client informed them the manager was not in fact racist. As they collectively breathed a sigh of relief, they continued reading and realized their manager was exhibiting behaviors that were classist. She was basically a snob. That distinction matters because it changed the development and education this manager needed.

Perspective and Belonging

Belonging is measured from the point of view of the person you want to ensure belongs, not from the perspective of the company leadership. How the company feels about what they're doing and what measures they're taking don't matter. What matters is the perception of the employees. Never has the phrase "perception is reality," been truer. It's a hard lesson to learn and an even tougher one to implement, but it is not impossible.

How Do You Create Belonging at Work?

Maslow's hierarchy of needs is a motivational theory that depicts five levels of needs that individuals must satisfy in order to reach higher-level growth needs. It isn't necessary for the levels to be completely satisfied in order for a person to progress, but what is interesting is that the need to belong is squarely in the middle. The idea that a person cannot be fully motivated to achieve without the sense of connectedness to others in the workplace demonstrates belonging isn't simply a new concept created by diversity and inclusion enthusiasts and that it is vital to maintaining a highly productive and profitable company.

The need to belong can be met by hosting events that build trust and connection, that offer ways for employees to create and maintain effective working relationships, and that support high levels of engagement among teams. It can also include:

- Using the office intranet to host a page for each employee and office so people can get to know each other and build their internal networks. When I worked at MUFG Americas, I contributed to growing their intranet through internal marketing and participation by ERGs.

- Hosting a celebratory lunch for your team so everyone can discuss their wins, whether that's a birthday, work anniversary, project completion, or birth of a child.

- Establishing meetings that aren't work related and for the purpose of getting to know one another.

- Meeting norms that include time to check in before diving straight into work. This helps you get a quick pulse of how everyone is feeling that day and increases team connection.

How Do You Identify Belonging?

Once you've offered up activities and tools to create belonging, measuring it is the next step. While there is no specific formula you can point to, one thing leaders can do to assess whether or not their employees have a sense of belonging is to look for behavior markers. For example, if you invite your team to an activity outside of work and one person is a perpetual no-show, it's clear that they don't feel like they belong. The onus is on the leader to decipher why that is. Is it an evening activity that would exclude a parent with small children at home? Are you meeting for drinks? Perhaps the individual has an aversion to alcohol? When you start to notice behavior patterns and begin to ask these questions, you'll be able to better decipher how to make your team members feel valued.

Surveys, as discussed in Chapter 6, are another opportunity to get a sense of how your employees are feeling. Even more important than the survey, however, is the follow-up. When a company has asked its employees to take the time to complete a survey, but never communicates the results or the proposed path forward, those employees won't feel valued and trust can't be established. You also will not be able to learn much about how employees are feeling.

We literally ask employees to rate the statement "I feel like I belong at XYZ Company," and when we see that only 33% "Agree" or "Strongly Agree," we know there is a big problem. The other questions in the survey help us learn what that problem might be. We always provide at least one opportunity for open-ended feedback. Obtaining feedback like the following examples can be tough to swallow, but it's necessary to learn what needs to be addressed:

- "This is the first job where I feel very alone and unwelcome."
- "Why do we do these surveys and then are never informed of the results?"
- "The environment is toxic, and it feels like everyone is disgruntled and management doesn't seem to notice or care."

As I've said throughout the book, it's pivotal for leaders to earn the trust of their employees across the board, but even more so when it comes to the efficacy of the diversity and inclusion process. When it comes to survey follow-up, something as simple as "We are working on these two areas and will get back to you soon" can bolster trust and keep the lines of communication open. If your employees can't trust your intentions or your follow-through, they'll never feel like they belong.

Another example of a comment includes: "This is a great place to work and I am proud to be a member of XYZ Company."

The good news is there are always bright spots to the work. It is never all doom and gloom, and that is what keeps us all moving forward with optimism that things can and will change for the better.

11

Unconscious Bias at Work

When companies say they would like to take action to deal with unconscious bias at work, they're usually referring to their recruiting and hiring process. Recruiters and talent acquisition professionals bear the brunt of the scrutiny when it comes to increasing diversity in the workplace. I've spoken with CEOs, directors of talent acquisition, human resource professionals, as well as individual recruiters and hiring managers, and what I have found is a disconnect between the goal of achieving diversity and the plan for getting there.

There is a misconception that if a company does not have a diverse employee population, it is because recruiters have been unable to identify diverse talent. Company leaders are quick to lay the blame at the feet of recruiters or on the diverse individuals themselves, by saying they aren't sufficiently qualified to apply.

The Most Qualified May Not Be the Right Candidate

It is common to hear hiring managers state they simply want to hire the most qualified person for the job. That statement, on its face, sounds so innocent and factual. Who doesn't want to hire the most qualified person for the job? However, that statement presupposes a number of things.

First, saying you want to hire the most qualified person for the job, but you systematically hire a white male every single time. This implies you really believe that every time, in every instance, for every job opening, a white male has been the best and most qualified candidate. Take a pause and reread that last sentence. Reflect on it for a moment and then tell me if you still believe there is no bias in your recruiting and hiring process.

Second, there is never usually only *one* most qualified person for the job. There are usually several individuals who are highly qualified and could do the job extremely well. How you decide between those highly qualified candidates is yet another place that unconscious bias is evident. In my course on unconscious bias, I discuss some of the more prevalent and pervasive forms of bias, such as affinity bias, groupthink, perception bias, the halo effect, confirmation bias, and gender bias.

Affinity Bias Favoring a candidate who shares a common interest, background, or experience with you.	**Example at work:** "I felt comfortable around her. I was just like her when I first started. She will be a great fit on my team."

Groupthink Agreeing with the majority opinion in order to fit in or because you don't want to be seen as difficult to work with.	**Example at work:** The candidate seemed like they could do the job and everyone else likes the person, so let's move forward with an offer even if you have genuine reservations about the candidate.
Perception Bias Making decisions based upon past assumptions instead of present evidence.	**Example at work:** You review the resume of a candidate from a school with a reputation for heavy drinking and lots of partying. You decide to pass on the candidate because you decide they will probably be less diligent and won't work as hard as everyone else on the team.
Halo Effect Seeing someone through a positive lens, even when there is evidence to the contrary.	**Example at work:** An employee always meets deadlines. However, after some time, they stop meeting deadlines, yet you continue to praise them as a model employee and make excuses for them.
Confirmation Bias A tendency to seek out people around us who will agree with us or data that confirms our opinion.	**Example at work:** You want to move a project forward and only pay attention to the data that supports your position.
Gender Bias Showing preference toward one gender over the other.	**Example at work:** You interview four men and one woman. The men have great conversations, discuss sports, and never really talk about their experience with the software you need them to know. You discuss the software with the woman and she stumbles over one explanation. After the interviews, you say the woman isn't qualified because of her slip-up.

Third, simply working hard and following the rules will ensure you get ahead. This meritocracy argument has to be dismantled. There is a bias toward hiring graduates from Ivy League schools, and in the legal field this practice is especially prominent. To get the top job at the highest-paying law firm, you have to graduate in the top 10% of your class and attend one of the best schools. In a meritocracy, everyone is evaluated on merit. However, this is flawed because for a meritocracy to work, everyone has to be objective and without bias of any kind.

A professor at MIT's Sloan School of Management explored how meritocracy and HR practices actually work in the workplace. In a study of 9,000 employees, it was revealed that despite stating that "performance is the primary basis for all salary increases," in actuality, women and underrepresented minorities had to work harder and achieve higher performance scores in order to receive the same salary increases as white men.

Setting Goals Equals Accountability

The plan for achieving diversity has to include goals. Most company leaders do not want to set targets for goals or be specific at all about how they are going to increase diversity because being specific creates accountability. Accountability requires action and action requires leadership.

The Need for Being Specific

When was the last time you accomplished something but were not specific about how you were going to get it done? The answer to that question is never. Never in the history of "doing" have you just thought about a task and it magically got accomplished by itself.

The main excuse leaders use for not being specific is that specificity equates to quotas. However, contrary to popular belief, people of color want to be recognized and hired for their skills and ability, just like everyone else. Quotas are disliked by people of color because nobody wants to work for a company that is being forced to hire them.

The plan for achieving diversity has to be specific because diversity counts the people. Numbers are always specific, and you have to know the demographics of your company in order to design a plan for how you are going to shift. That does not mean that you are going to make an edict that you must hire 20 women over the next two months. However, you can put a process in place for increasing the number of women in your pipeline by analyzing the effectiveness of the sources you use to recruit women from, improving the brand marketing that you use to attract women to your company, and understanding the demographic makeup of the surrounding community where these women will ultimately work.

Watch for a Lack of Buy-In

Unconscious bias in the recruiting process is apparent in the lack of buy-in from leaders. There is no alignment to the creation of a process for increasing diversity because many leaders are unsure they can be successful due to their bias and their belief in the narrative that there are no highly qualified diverse individuals.

This is compounded by their belief that diversity recruiting is unnecessary because if you simply hire the best person, qualified diverse candidates will just rise to the top automatically *if* they are the most qualified.

Finally, many leaders don't actually want to take any action. They just want to talk about the issue and appear as though they plan to do something about it but continue along with business as usual because they enjoy the status quo, and it is working for them.

And before you take issue with what I have said, consider the example of a friend of mine who is a teacher. She has a number of students in her class who speak English as a second language or come from lower socioeconomic backgrounds. Most of those students are Black or Latino. Since she teaches in middle school, she is not their only teacher, but in her role, she works to keep the parents involved and to provide them with information they need. When a student is falling behind, she reaches out and interacts with the parent to ensure they understand how their child can get caught up and she is able to get the work completed by the student. However, many of the other teachers can't be bothered to do that. They'd rather talk about it and appear as if they're doing their job. In staff meetings, when a particular student's name comes up, the teachers will discuss the student and talk about how lazy the student is and lament that they never turn in their work. They all sigh, and then they move on with their day.

But my friend will break the status quo. She will ask the teachers what they have done to get the work. She lets them know that she took the time to send an email and was able to obtain completed assignments. Or she uses Google translate to make the assignment easier to understand.

So, I ask you, what have you done to reach the goal? What have you done to increase diversity in your workplace? Or are you like these teachers who enjoy complaining, who really think they are doing their jobs, but in fact are content to sit in status quo. In 2017, when Google announced they were launching Google for Jobs, their reasoning was because the problem is people can't find jobs. What I've seen—and what professionals of color know—is that the problem isn't *finding* a job; the problem is getting hired.

Let's look at what you can do to tackle unconscious bias in your workplace and reduce the barriers to entry.

Recruiting and Hiring

Talent acquisition, as a department, has high visibility within a company, which is one reason it is the first place that leaders direct their attention when attempting to increase the diversity of the workforce.

Workplace Culture Starts with Leaders

Recruiters may not be the final decision makers when selecting a candidate to hire, but they definitely play a large part. They are the first live point of contact for a candidate so what they say, their attitude, and how they respond to candidates (or their lack of response) sets the tone for the hiring process from the perspective of the candidate and begins to create an impression of the workplace culture and probability of belonging.

However, when we focus on recruiters, we forget about their other half – the hiring manager. A recruiter recruits because a hiring manager needs to hire, so when a recruiter seeks talent with specific skills or experience levels, those requirements are set by the hiring manager. You may recall a rather high-profile case of a recruiter who was fired for posting a job with the requirement of "white preferred." No one talks about the hiring manager who made that ask or a culture that allows such an ask to be made. Firing the recruiter didn't change anything. Diversity didn't increase, workplace culture didn't improve, inclusion doesn't exist, and belonging is unattainable.

When I work with company leaders to provide unconscious bias education for the talent acquisition team, I usually insist we offer education for hiring managers too. One particular client comes to mind whose CEO challenged me on the rationale of this tactic.

As we discussed the challenges the talent acquisition team was having in relation to the company diversity goals, the CEO told me it is the job of the head of talent acquisition to make sure diversity goals are reached. He literally said that she needed to "make it happen." I agreed with him, then added that the talent acquisition team doesn't actually do the hiring and asked what the talent acquisition team is supposed to do when the hiring managers ignore their advice. He responded that the heads of those departments that are hiring need to handle that. So I kept going, and I asked who the head of each department reports to. He paused before answering and you could see the lightbulb go off when he realized his part in all of it. At that moment he realized he had been tasking talent acquisition with fixing problems outside of their department.

Recruiters and Managers Working Together

Recruiters do have the ability to influence the decision-making process. When recruiters and hiring managers work together, instead of creating a hostile or adversarial relationship, the recruiter can use their expertise to appropriately advise and coach the hiring manager.

Some of the ways a recruiter can do this is by probing to understand the thinking of the hiring manager. What is their ultimate goal? What are they attempting to achieve? Ask:

- I see that you have three finalists. One is male, and he was referred. One is female and all things being equal, can we hire the woman?

- I noticed that you haven't made a diverse hire in months. Can we partner to improve your success in this area?

- You mentioned that you are trying to hire for fit. What does that look like to you? How do you define a "good fit" for this role? What about "fit" for your team/location/department are you looking for?
- You mentioned that you like to hire candidates from _____ University. What specific skills do those candidates possess that make them stand out?

Job Descriptions

Just like the images on your website give people an idea of what your company values and finds important, your job descriptions can do the same thing. When thinking about diversity and recruiting, DEI strategists focus on the job description. Words are powerful and can paint a picture of a workplace that ultimately deters diverse people from applying. Job descriptions can be subtly discriminatory across many dimensions; however, research shows that gender-biased language seems to be the most prevalent.

According to a study published in the *Journal of Personality and Social Psychology*, we have learned that unconscious bias in job descriptions often leads to women opting out from applying for jobs. The study also found that, while masculine wording in job descriptions did discourage women from applying, descriptions that included feminine language did little to dissuade men from applying for jobs. The study, entitled "Evidence That Gendered Wording in Job Advertisements Exists and Sustains Gender Inequality," is the work of three researchers who took the time to explore the link between job ads and gender bias and why women continue to be underrepresented in traditionally male-dominated industries. Their work underscores the idea that words do matter.

What you write and how you portray a job opening affects the person who decides to apply. Here is an example of a question I received from a contact on LinkedIn:

We are currently hiring for a senior role, and out of 100+ applications more than 95% are from men! Is our job description gender biased?

I won't identify the company or the job description they sent me, but I'll share my feedback, which I was able to provide in under five minutes and that includes my time spent reviewing the job description. I first read the description and then I immediately went to the "About Us" page on their company website. My response to the individual who reached out, in part, was as follows:

The required prior industry experience on your job description are all from traditionally male-centric industries. If the candidate must have experience in one of those industries, it is highly likely that you are going to identify men for the posted job. Additionally, what do you see in the two photos I've attached?

In the first photo I attached, there were snapshots of people who work for the company. Every single face was a white man. The second photo was a screen capture of a video on their website that starts with two men climbing a mountain and two additional older white men smiling at a conference table.

You may be wondering, why does it matter? So what if there are men in the photos? Why wouldn't women want to apply? Why would they feel left out? Consider that Ruth Bader Ginsburg said, "When I'm sometimes asked when will there be enough [women on the Supreme Court] and I say, 'When there are nine,' people are shocked. But there'd been nine men, and nobody's ever raised a question about that."

If it is perfectly fine to have the Supreme Court filled with men, why not the opposite? If that doesn't seem right to you – therein lies the bias. If you wouldn't consider asking your marketing team to remove every appearance of a man and replace them with women, there is the problem. If it's not okay in the reverse, why do we allow the status quo to remain?

Implicit bias takes the form of certain word associations and may look like the following:

- Nurse = female
- Software engineer = male
- Lego bricks = toys for boys
- Barbie dolls = toys for girls

The gendered wording research study explained there are ways to improve your job descriptions to increase the number of women interested in a job you are attempting to fill. Here is an example of how:

Average Description of an Engineering Firm: We are a dominant engineering firm that boasts many leading clients. We are determined to stand apart from the competition.

BETTER: We are a community of engineers who have effective relationships with many satisfied clients. We are committed to thoroughly understanding the engineering sector.

Here you can see that I removed several masculine words, including "dominant," "boasts," "determined," and "competition." Instead, I added "community," "relationships," and "understanding."

Average Description of Qualifications: Self-sufficient, independent worker, with an ability to perform in a competitive environment. Confident to manage customer expectations and meet company goals.

BETTER: Understanding team dynamics, has an ability to be proficient at managing expectations and collaborating to ensure team success. Maintain great client relations.

Average Description of Responsibilities: Competently direct project groups to manage progress and ensure accurate task control. Lead project in compliance with clients' objectives.

BETTER: Working interdependently, provide general support to project team. Create a cohesive working relationship with project team while ensuring team goals are met.

In the description of qualifications and responsibilities, similar, more traditionally masculine words were removed and replaced. This is not the only way to rewrite these descriptions. You can get creative. Keep the purpose in mind. Are you writing the job description with the idea of making it neutral or are you attempting to attract a different dimension of diversity? It will take some time to research and find words that will help attract the individuals you are seeking, and it wouldn't hurt to test them with the target demographic before finalizing.

In addition to the job description, the following information should be highly visible on your career portal or in links in the job description:

- The organization's vision, mission, and values
- Short description of the company's products and/or services
- Explanation of benefits
- Steps in the selection process
- Videos that give a realistic view of the company; could include tours of the workplace and/or videos of current employees explaining why they work there

Resume Blind Spots

A resume is filled with biased blind spots and will challenge you the most when it comes to reducing areas of bias in the hiring process. Each of the following areas is a minefield of its own.

Candidate Name

Numerous studies have shown that a name on a resume can have a significant impact on whether the candidate is screened out from the process.

When reviewing resumes, pause and ask yourself if the reservation or the desire to advance the candidate to an interview with the hiring manager is based upon any perceived bias around their name. If you've ever attended one of my sessions for recruiters that discusses unconscious bias or if you have watched my LinkedIn Learning course on Diversity Recruiting, you've probably heard me talk about José Zamora. José was featured in a BuzzFeed article because he discussed his inability to get a job. He explained how he applied to more than 100 jobs and could not get even a single call back. However, after he decided to change his name to Joe on his resume, he got lots of callbacks and even job offers. He didn't change anything else on his resume other than removing the "s" from his first name.

College Attended

Much emphasis is placed on the university a candidate attended and if they do not have a degree at all, should it really be required? This is an area that should be discussed at the beginning of the process with the hiring manager so that you can have the broadest pool available to you. Upon having a conversation with the candidate, you might find they have a second degree at the university that you consider to be top notch.

Sometimes bias is so ingrained that getting past it is difficult. A few years ago, one of the consultants I work with was on a project with a client who had a desire to increase the diversity of their candidate pool. Her suggestion was for the client to recruit from additional schools and she suggested some Historically Black Colleges and Universities (HBCUs). They liked the idea and followed through by sending their recruiting team to a career fair at an HBCU. When the consultant followed up to ask how it went, the client was excited. They mentioned that they increased their gender diversity because they hired two women and a man. The consultant asked about diversity of race and ethnicity because that was why she suggested an HBCU and the client said they hired three white individuals. Statistically, I'm not even sure how that is possible. This is why we spend more time defining diversity when working with clients because the client in this instance was thinking about gender diversity while the consultant was working to increase diversity of both gender and race.

Prior Employer

Where an employee has previously worked can be used as a culture check to:

- Align with company size to learn how a candidate handled a company similar to yours.
- Determine whether the product sold and sales cycle is similar to yours.

However, be careful that you are comparing apples to apples. Sometimes, one department in a large company can have a very different culture from another. Don't assume you understand the culture someone is leaving based purely upon the company name.

Also, don't get caught up in the incestuous cycle that many industries fall into – if you're a tech company you like to hire individuals who worked at well-known tech companies or if you are a well-known tech company, the employees have all worked at Apple, Google, Microsoft, IBM, or Dell at some point in their career. If someone in tech hasn't worked at one of these companies, but you only like to hire individuals who have worked at one of these companies, how would they ever get hired?

Think back to my example of the hiring manager who asked me if his job description was gender biased and the first thing I noticed was the requirement for the applicants to be from a specific list of male-centric industries. What is the point of entry? Stop making it difficult for others who are just as qualified, but your procedures don't allow the opportunity for the candidate to demonstrate it.

City of Residence

If hiring is part of your responsibility, at some point you've looked at a resume and discarded it because the applicant lived too far away from your office. It is not your job to make the determination of how far a commute is too far. Once you speak to the candidate, you may find that they are in the process of moving closer to your office. It is also likely that with the high cost of living in the area, a candidate may have to travel further than what you think is acceptable. However, the candidate may be used to traveling a further distance for work. Do not judge what is "normal" or acceptable for someone else.

Gaps in Experience

Do not assume a gap in the resume of a candidate automatically denotes something negative. There are many reasons for a gap that don't diminish the professional experience a candidate brings to the table.

- Taking time off to travel
- Taking time to care for a family member, or for their own health (including pregnancy)
- Attending school full-time
- Taking a sabbatical
- Having a medical procedure
- Other reasons that are none of your business and don't affect their ability to do the job

Job Hopping

If you see that a candidate has many short-term jobs or has been a contract employee for many years, look at the circumstances. Were they in short-term, contract roles because that was helpful to their lifestyle at the time? Keep in mind that underrepresented individuals are much more likely to get stuck in contract roles and not given an opportunity for permanent full-time work because they are dealing with the bias that comes from these types of roles as well as the fact that, being an underrepresented individual, there is a bias that they're in that role because they aren't as qualified and are less likely to be given a chance to prove otherwise. If the moves were between permanent jobs, look at the time frame. Was this during a recession? Again, underrepresented individuals are more likely to be let go when layoffs occur and only hired into contract roles when the economy begins to rebound. Are you perpetuating that cycle?

Employee Referals

Studies have shown that 65% to 75% of jobs in the United States are filled through employee referrals, or networking. Combine that with the fact that referred employees have a nearly 50% retention rate after two years and you see why there is a focus on referred candidates.

When sourcing for diversity, it is important to emphasize employee referrals and recruiting efforts within diverse individuals and communities because until demographics within your organization change, referred candidates are unlikely to be diverse, so it will be necessary to minimize the extent to which you prioritize referrals over other candidates.

To improve the diversity of employee referrals, hiring managers and recruiters should focus on building relationships with contacts at HBCUs, within Employee Resource Groups (ERGs), and with external industry associations and professional organizations. For a non-exhaustive list, see the Resources section.

Interviewing

You can work to mitigate the negative impact of bias on your organization's decision-making in the interview process by implementing a structured interviewing process. Most companies spend a significant amount of time talking about how to achieve diverse candidate slates, but not nearly as much time is spent ensuring there are diverse interviewer slates. One in five women report they are often the only woman in the room at work. They are more likely to have their abilities challenged, be subject to unprofessional remarks, and are 1.5 times more likely to think about leaving their jobs than women who are not the sole woman in the room.[1]

There are ways you can prevent placing a burden on an "Only" in the interviewing process.

- Have a candid discussion with hiring managers and support them in building relationships with individuals around the organization, both inside and outside of their department. This way when they ask a diverse individual to participate in an interview, it won't be the first or even the second time they're having a conversation.

- Work with your ERGs to nominate individuals who can participate in the process. Rotating responsibility prevents one or two individuals being overly tasked with this role, which is over and above the responsibilities of their job.

- If you consistently have a problem identifying diverse individuals to participate as part of your interview panel and don't have an ERG, this is demonstrative of the challenge you are seeking to address. Create a schedule, rotate women and other "Only's" so they are not unduly burdened with supporting the recruitment and hiring efforts, and don't only acknowledge but reward their participation and commitment to helping your organization meet its diversity goals.

---

[1]L.A. Rivera, "Hiring as Cultural Matching"; R.E. Steinpreis, K.A. Anders, and D. Ritzke, "The Impact of Gender on the Review of Curricula Vitae of Job Applicants and Tenure Candidates"; Moss-Racusin, Dovidio, Brescoll, et al., "Science Faculty's Subtle Gender Biases Favor Male Students"; L.A. Rudman, C.A. Moss-Racusin, P. Glick, and J.E. Phelan, "Reactions to Vanguards."

The external perception created regarding how diverse candidates are treated internally can be a significant factor in attracting diverse applicants. When the only company representatives to speak on panels, be present at interviews, or talk about the company products are majority group members, it may send a subtle message to members of underrepresented groups that they do not belong in the company and may not be successful there. Representation matters. To be even more specific, authentic representation matters. Representation without authenticity will be perceived as tokenism.

During the Interview

When questions are consistent across candidates, bias has been found to be reduced over and above unstructured or free-form interviews.[2] Using structured interviews helps to keep the questions focused on the main purpose of the job as well as the key responsibilities. It requires taking time to adequately prepare for the interview not by reviewing the resume of the person, but by understanding what the key skills and requirements are for the successful candidate. Too often, hiring managers spend a few moments prior to the interview skimming the resume and then dive right into the interview. To reduce bias in the process it is important to use the standard process every time, with every candidate.

A job scorecard can help maintain consistency by providing a standard document on which to maintain focus on the position you are filling, and the requirements and skills needed to make a competent and less biased evaluation. A job scorecard allows you to rate each candidate using standard metrics that are created for the specific job. By allowing each interviewer not only to rate but

---

[2] J.D. Bragger, E. Kutcher, J. Morgan, et al. "The Effects of the Structured Interview on Reducing Biases Against Pregnant Job Applicants," Sex Roles 46 (2002): 215–226.

also to record feedback in a clear and objective way, the emphasis is on the skills, traits, and key competencies needed for the specific job rather than relying on the gut feel of the interviewer.

Using a job scorecard, combined with structured interviews, will help reduce bias in the process. Your job is to find a way to include the person, not exclude them. Our focus has been all wrong for far too long. Instead of looking to identify reasons the candidate might not measure up, focus on finding reasons you want to hire the person.

Sample Questions to Ask

Ask questions that provide an opportunity for the candidate to list their accomplishments and achievements from their past. For example:

- "How do you see this job fitting into your future career plans?"
- "Give me an example of a time you set a goal and then achieved it."

Then listen for alignment with your company's values. Do they link their skills and attributes to ways that will benefit your company?

Ask questions that demonstrate a desire for continuous learning and embracing of evolving trends. For example:

- "If you were unsure how to complete a task within your role, how would you figure it out?"
- "What type of professional development activities have you participated in over the past two years?"

Then listen for ways in which they have sought out exploration, new ideas, and opportunities for continuous learning.

Ask questions that provide an opportunity for the candidate to demonstrate their ability to be inclusive and be collaborative at work. For example:

- "Describe a situation where you have had to work with someone who is doing something that you do not agree with due to cultural or style differences. How did you approach the situation?"
- "Tell about a time when your active listening skills really paid off, perhaps a situation when others missed a key idea or issue."

Then listen for ways in which they used communication skills and demonstrated empathy.

Scoring and Evaluating

Your use of the candidate scorecard and subsequent evaluation of the candidate will profoundly influence the hiring decisions. Therefore, as you score the answers:

- Ensure the rubric you use is standard for each candidate for the role.
- Define in advance what great answers, decent answers, and poor answers look like for each question.
- Continue to use the rubric when discussing the candidate with others on the interview panel.
- Ensure everyone on your team is using the same rubric.

Onboarding

Empathy is an underrated trait as a leader. Do you remember your first day of a new job? Imagine you arrive at the front desk and are greeted this way by someone in the company: "Oh, hello . . . I forgot you were coming today."

When I was a hiring manager at Prudential, I would have to ensure we onboarded our new hires. And every time we had a new hire, I would cringe because due to protocols, we couldn't order a laptop for the new hire until their first day of work but it would take three business days for their laptop to arrive once ordered, so the new employee would be unable to access any systems, do any work, check email, or feel like part of the team for nearly a week until their laptop arrived. Before I was promoted, a new hire wouldn't even know where they were going to sit when they arrived on their first day, and many times their manager wasn't even present to welcome them to work. What type of impression do you think that gave to a new hire? How long do you think they lasted under those conditions?

Whether it's forgotten paperwork, technology, or even an arrival, what happens in these situations is demoralizing. Our onboarding process is directly tied to our company's culture, and when you add in a lack of diversity on top of it, the first impression of your company is not a good one. Nearly one-third of new hires become dissatisfied with their job and will begin to seek new employment within the first six months of a job,[3] so retention is a key benefit of good onboarding.

When recruiting for diversity, it is especially important to have an onboarding system that actually helps onboard and reduces bias. Examples include creating a team of diverse individuals to welcome the new hires. By ensuring the team is diverse, the new hire has a choice of who they'd like to speak with. Ensuring they are diverse not only in race, ethnicity, gender, and sexual orientation but in tenure with the organization and in function

---

[3]https://www.gartner.com/smarterwithgartner/category/human-resources.

provides the new hire with the opportunity to learn about ongoing projects they may have to join, acronyms they need to know, important clients they should be up to speed on, as well as the fun stuff like favorite restaurants to visit at lunch time.

Creating a sense of belonging using a process that is both relational and technical will help new employees feel comfortable working in proximity to one other, not as individuals who are fending for themselves but as a team working for a common goal.

The technical process is where new hires learn the company – the ins and outs, the organizational chart, acronyms, and the lingo used around the office. It should also include specifics on important clients, so they are up to speed and can hit the ground running. Pinterest is a company that does the technical aspect well. During their week-long orientation they schedule time for company leadership talks, IT setup, and other essential needs for success – which should be the goal of every onboarding process: getting the newest hire to the greatest level of success as quickly as possible. The relational aspect focuses on team building and creating lasting relationships.

As you work to reduce bias in your practices, policies, and procedures at work, the goal should be to answer these questions:

- Diversity asks: How many more diverse hires do we have this year than last year?
- Inclusion asks: How many of the diverse hires did we retain?
- Equity asks: What procedures have we put in place to create conditions where *everyone* can thrive, not just the majority group?
- Belonging asks: Do all employees feel like they belong with us, not just work for us?

12

Leaders See Color

But I'm not racist.

It's a declaration I hear all too often, used as a signal that the policy we're discussing or the action being taken shouldn't be considered harmful because the individual who followed the policy or took the action isn't personally racist.

In one example, it was uttered by a CEO whom I had just informed that an employee, John, had been accused several times of using racial slurs and discriminatory jokes in the workplace. Regardless of those complaints, John was promoted to director of sales, sending the message that the company doesn't actually value all of its employees in the same way.

What this CEO failed to understand was that his inaction to address the complaints against John, and his decision to promote him despite them, communicates to his employees that he approves of John's behavior or, at the very least, that it's less important to him than John's ability to bolster the company's bottom line.

Choosing Anti-Racism

We tend to think that not discriminating is enough. However, there's a vast difference between not being racist and being anti-racist. Anti-racism is the active process of identifying and eliminating racism by changing systems, organizational structures, policies, practices, and attitudes. "I'm not racist" is just semantics, but anti-racism is taking action to force change.

Sometimes anti-racism means jumping right in to flip company policies on their heads, but sometimes it's initiating uncomfortable conversations in the workplace that have previously been considered taboo. We've been told that topics like race, religion, and politics are too controversial, and therefore inappropriate around the water cooler. However, the time has come for us to stop holding on to what is considered "acceptable" at work.

I often use the television show *Madmen* to illustrate this concept. The show depicts an advertising agency in the 1950s, when it was considered acceptable for men to make inappropriate comments or slap the behind of a female coworker. Today, that kind of behavior is fodder for a major lawsuit. Even more recent is the evolution of work in 2020, where CEOs of major companies conducted meetings over Zoom from their bedrooms. What is considered acceptable in the workplace is completely contingent on the circumstances of the time, and is therefore always changing.

While discussing race at work may have previously been frowned upon, 2020 has made it blatantly clear that it's a discussion we all need to get comfortable with having. Avoidance is not the answer. If you really want to lessen the effects of bias, you can no longer ignore it or avoid talking about it. You're going to have to deal with it head on and get past it.

Using Descriptors Over Labels

One of my many jobs was working for one of the largest law firms in New York City. When one of my coworkers was describing someone on our floor, he kept saying, "You know him. He's tall, has dark hair, has a beard. I've seen you talking to him. He's in marketing, and he hangs out with John from accounting."

I couldn't figure out who he was talking about and he was beginning to get frustrated. But after what seemed like forever, I finally figured out who he meant. And then *I* began to feel frustrated. I asked him, "Why didn't you just say he's Black?"

Awkward!

People trip over themselves to avoid using race as a descriptor. We avoid it because we don't want to inadvertently say something that will offend someone else. Where people tend to stray down a dangerous path is by leading with race rather than leading with the person.

In our education sessions with employees, I give these two examples:

- Do you know the Black woman who works in marketing?
- Do you know Stacey? She works in marketing, she's got curly hair, and she's Black.

Too often, we use the first example and not the second.

As subtle as this difference is, it makes all the difference in the world. One is a label, the other is a descriptor.

There's a vast difference between seeing and acknowledging color, and judging, assuming, and basing decisions about someone purely because of it.

Every time I use this example in a session, at least one person will come up to me afterward and tell me how eye-opening it was and how helpful it is because they have fumbled over this for most of their lives. When you are behaving awkwardly because you're doing your very best not to mention race, it makes it painfully obvious that you are trying very hard not to mention race. And *that* is what puts you in a less than favorable light.

Other examples include:

- "Have you met the disabled woman," versus "Have you met Anna; she uses a wheelchair?"
- "Do you know the gay guy in accounting?" versus "Do you know John in accounting?"

Avoiding Race Is Not a Solution

Leaders understand that color exists in their workplace. Have you ever uttered the words "I don't see color"?

- "I don't see color" is harmful.
- "I don't see color" is dismissive.
- "I don't see color" is an act of denial.

Too often as a rebuttal I hear, "But Stacey, didn't Dr. Martin Luther King say he wanted his children to live in a world where they would be judged by the content of their character, not by the color of their skin?" My response is yes, definitely. But notice he said judged. He didn't say not to see the color. He simply said stop judging people based upon it.

If you ever want to observe how quickly the temperature of a room can get chilly, start talking about race or religion. There are some strongly held beliefs about both, so it's no wonder there's a feeling that when discussing race, saying you "don't see color" is a safe way to go.

However, this line of thinking couldn't be more wrong. There's a reason people who are not white will never utter that phrase. Speaking as a Black woman, I value my individual differences. Everyone wants to be recognized for their individuality, but we don't want to be singled out or treated differently at work because we're a woman or because we have a disability. It's why you cannot treat color blindness and gender blindness in the same way. As with everything to do with diversity and inclusion, there is nuance involved. I am a Black woman who is proud to be both female and Black and, yes, I would like you to acknowledge that. But I don't expect to be denied a job because of it. I don't expect to be paid less because of it, and I don't expect to be stuck at a lower level in the company because of it.

Addressing Labels

It is necessary for us to confront the issue of labeling. I've been asked so many questions about when to use the term "African American" versus "Black," whether we should say "Latino" or "Hispanic," and whether the term "gay" is still okay or if you should use "LGBTQ+." My answer to this is always ask. I can't know the ethnicity of every single person on the planet, nor can I know whether my friend who is from Guatemala prefers to be called Guatemalan or Latina. If I ask, I can get it right 100% of the time. When I don't ask, I have a 50/50 shot at being wrong.

After an education session on diversity for a national association, a white woman came up to me and seemed rather frustrated. She said she tried to speak to one of her Black coworkers about diversity and the Black woman got angry. So now she, the white woman, didn't know what else to do and decided she wasn't going to talk about diversity-related topics anymore. As an alternative, I simply suggested she talk to someone else about it.

It can seem like such a simple step, but really, if you and a coworker were talking about coffee in the break room and the person got angry, would you decide never to talk about coffee again? Of course not. You might watch what you say around that particular person, but you won't strike coffee from your list of small-talk topics. So why is it that if you speak to someone about a subject that is arguably more tense than coffee, you come to the logical conclusion that the subject is never to be discussed again?

Likewise, I would counsel the person who got angry to look back on their actions and determine if they could have handled the conversation better. Raising awareness isn't all about the other person. Sometimes it is as much about you being aware that someone else is attempting to understand as it is about them understanding.

The level of discomfort you have about discussing race is projected outward and other people feel that. So the next time you want to shy away from including race in the discussion, don't. By becoming more comfortable, not only can you begin to reduce your own bias, but you can begin to reduce the unintended consequences of avoidance.

Having Hard Conversations

Rather than being taught that we shouldn't talk about things like race, politics, or religion at work, we should have been taught *how* to talk about these things by our elders. By avoiding them altogether, we find ourselves at a point in our history when these discussions are absolutely necessary but, with no frame of reference for these kinds of conversations, we are without the tools that facilitate healthy, respectful discussions.

That being said, while I *am* encouraging you to stop avoiding these conversations, I am *not* suggesting that you rip the band-aid right off and engage the first person of color you see in the grocery store. Following the events of George Floyd's death, a group of Black women had expressed to me that they were tired of acquaintances asking them questions about being Black, lamenting that it wasn't their responsibility to educate white people. As we continued to talk, it became less about answering the interrogative questions of others, and more about how the lack of a relationship with these particular people made it impossible to know their true motives in asking.

Hard conversations can only land softly if there's a foundational relationship already laid. Topics like race, religion, and politics are incredibly personal, so venturing into those waters without any established connection or trust will be fruitless at best and destructive at worst. Building trust is challenging because it takes time and effort, but it's also simple in that it only requires you to slow down enough to check in with people and listen when they talk.

I once presented a workshop on the afternoon of an all-day, online conference. Before the session started, I greeted participants with a private message asking how their day was going. For the most part, I got the typical, one-word responses, but one woman shared that her best friend had unexpectedly died that morning. It was the first time she had shared the news with anyone, because it took until mid-afternoon before anyone even asked her how she was doing. Imagine working all day and not feeling comfortable to share news that is greatly affecting your mood and your productivity? Or maybe you don't have to imagine because you are one of the many individuals who do this regularly.

Building connections is as simple as checking in with people on a regular basis and earnestly listening to what's going on in their lives. Over time, as trust builds, hard conversations can be broached more easily because the other person will have a better sense of your motivation and authenticity in asking difficult questions. They'll feel less like they are being interrogated by the opposition, and more like they are being understood by an ally.

Allies Drive Change Forward

Simply defined, an ally is someone who supports another in an ongoing effort. As previously mentioned, people don't become allies overnight. It takes time, effort, and intentionality to build the trust required to earn the title. In order for leaders to make real changes in the diversity and inclusiveness of their organization, they have to become allies first. Leaders who strive to connect with their team cultivate an office culture that values the sharing of all ideas and the provision of honest feedback – a culture with the freedom and space to innovate.

An ally can show up as someone whose support includes:

- Taking action to confront and combat racism
- Speaking up when you see discrimination, bias, racism, and inequality
- Taking part in equality
- Offering support to empower those affected by systemic racism
- Using your platforms, voice, and influence to draw attention to examples of racial injustice to demand and create change

Being an ally is active. Allyship, on the other hand, is passive, although equally important for leaders. Allyship is a form of support that includes:

- Listening to BIPOCs (Black, Indigenous, and People of Color) talk about their experiences and learning from them

- Educating yourself about race and how systemic racism creates and perpetuates inequality
- Educating others
- Modeling inclusivity
- Self-reflection
- Committing to continuous improvement

Understanding the concepts of allyship and how to be an ally as a leader is very important, because you need to know the history of diversity and inclusion in order to do so. You will be challenged by others who don't understand what it is that you are doing and you will need to have the strength of your conviction in order to explain and defend your decisions. If you don't believe in what you're doing, why would anyone else?

Looking Back to Move Forward

Speaking as a Black woman in America, during the time of the passage of the Civil Rights Act of 1964, the goal was for us to ensure we did not stand out if we had the opportunity to get a job in a professional environment, though it was very difficult. The workplace culture was largely homogeneously white and male. As a reminder, the Civil Rights Act of 1964 was put in place to criminalize discrimination on the basis of race, color, religion, sex, or national origin. Discrimination may have been illegal on paper, but it was not enforced in the workplace, which is why affirmative action policies came into play (see Chapter 8).

With the passage of time, women and Black professionals transitioned from being excluded in the workplace to attempting to actively fit in and assimilate. This is where diversity efforts began from the compliance standpoint. The goal was to ensure that the company was in compliance with these new laws and wasn't concerned with the thoughts or opinions of the employees this impacted. Employee engagement surveys were definitely not happening. No one was asking or cared whether women felt included or safe at work.

However, as gender diversity initiatives began to increase, diversity initiatives that focused on race and ethnicity also saw an increase. There was conversation around multiculturalism and cultural sensitivity as we began to celebrate differences and recognize visible diversity.

Focusing on Inclusion as an Ally

We are now in the period of time where there is a focus on inclusion. We have recognized that diversity is a measurement, but inclusion is the mechanism for creating a positive workplace culture and you cannot be successful as an ally without recognizing this fact. Allies are needed to help traditionally marginalized individuals overcome the hurdles and the barriers that have prevented them from speaking up for themselves.

Speak Up to Create Change

As an ally, what is expected of you is the action – the affirmative action that you can individually take in your workplace. Have you been in a meeting and heard something you didn't think was quite right? Did you second-guess yourself and think, "They couldn't have meant that the way it sounded?" Did you decide not to say anything because you didn't want to cause a scene or, worse yet, get the person who said it in trouble?

Allies can create cultures where everyone is comfortable speaking up and to do that, we have to change the way we speak to each other, about each other, and on behalf of each other.

You've heard the saying "If you don't have anything nice to say, say nothing at all." That doesn't apply when you have something true but uncomfortable to say. It doesn't mean you should only speak up when you have flattering things to say and it's not supposed to keep you from disagreeing with others.

Our problem really is in communicating uncomfortable facts. We're terrible at it and so we avoid it at all costs.

Listening and Action

Allies let their peers and employees know they are not only willing to listen, but also will act appropriately upon the information shared. Saying something only happens when we think someone is going to hear us.

A coworker was in a staff meeting when someone decided to use an inappropriate word to describe a gay person. She used the word several times in this meeting and it made him very uncomfortable. He thought if he noticed it, others must have also.

What added to his discomfort was the fact that they had just hired a new staff member who was gay and he thought it was suspect that, all of a sudden, derogatory remarks against gay people were being mentioned in their meeting, so he reported it to HR. The next time it happened, he also spoke up and said those types of comments wouldn't be tolerated in their meetings. He was able to do that because they had a culture that made all employees feel supported; their workforce was diverse and was accepting of everyone. Can your company say the same?

Allies work to review current policies to ensure they encourage people to speak up and allow for the uncomfortable conversations that will ultimately arise. Allies address these potential issues in staff meetings, town halls, and department briefings. Allies make it clear that they will no longer stand by and ignore a lack of consequences for behavior that is inconsistent with policies.

You may not want to speak up because you don't want to say the wrong thing; say it anyway. Identify areas for growth and learning and lean in.

It may be uncomfortable, and you might not like confrontation, but you don't have to be confrontational to confront inequity. Use your ability to influence to educate others.

Leaders, as allies, model the behavior they expect to see. How might you show your support as an ally within your company? How might you talk to a colleague about their less than supportive behavior when discussing diversity, equity, and inclusion in the workplace? What are some steps you can take to create a more diverse and inclusive team?

Advocacy

13

Driving Change

There are three layers to driving change and making it stick. Leaders are appropriately successful at looking outward to two of the layers and driving change within their team and their company, but when it comes to self-reflection and looking inward, it is there we find the most resistance.

Change takes courage and it's easy to challenge others on their behaviors and point out what's wrong with company policies, but when it comes time to see how we might ourselves be contributing to the problem, we avoid that level of feedback. Taking personal responsibility for the outcomes makes us committed to achieving our goals. It also makes us accountable and it improves our odds of success.

It is why the hiring of a Chief Diversity Officer should be done with full transparency that the job of the CDO is to partner with leadership in the implementation of a DEI strategy, not to be the only owner and driver of an initiative.

In June 2020, I penned an article for *Fast Company* magazine that addressed some of the "check the box" activities that companies employ. Measure how many women we have in leadership – check! Attend a career fair at a school with higher diversity than our traditional universities we visit – check! Add the only Black person in management to our diversity committee – check! Unfortunately, when it comes to ensuring there is accountability for embedding diversity and inclusion into company actions, senior leaders begin pointing fingers at one another as each one attempts to shirk responsibility. As I stated in the article, "In the best of circumstances, companies hire a diversity and inclusion leader, put them in charge of all diversity and inclusion, give them no power, no resources, but do present them with a boatload of expectations and expect miracles."

Building Change

The following three features show three examples of senior diversity and inclusion roles that have crossed my desk just within the last week. As you review them, what are the first things you notice? Look at the level of responsibility and accountability. Pay attention to the qualifications required.

Director of Diversity and Community

How You'll Make a Difference

We are on a mission to build community both inside and out through high-quality products, services, and experiences that bring people together. As the Director of Diversity and

Community, you'll work to ensure an authentic sense of belonging for all, allow our business to do good in the communities we serve, and also help to tell the stories that keep our team connected and engaged.

We are committed to elevating our approach to diversity and belonging, so this role will be critical in helping to expand our thinking on people practices spanning recruitment, to performance management and volunteerism, to recognition. Ours is a team dedicated to recognizing and celebrating each other's humanity and we believe that when people can bring their whole selves to work, feel seen and safe, they can achieve their highest potential. We also recognize that systemic issues require systemic solutions and have begun the challenging but necessary work to lead by example to ensure our team is representative of our customers and the world.

Our business has always valued giving back and making sure that our teams are well-connected. We believe these efforts go hand in hand with our vision for a fully inclusive company. With that, the leadership of our existing volunteer team and our communications team will live within this role as well. This positioning will mean you'll champion progressive change management around diversity, equity, and belonging; enable team and business results; and maximize our collective ability to do good in the communities where we live and work. In short, you'll be the face of the company's diversity and community impact goals. In this role, you'll join the HR Leadership Team and will report directly to our SVP.

What You'll Do

This role is new for the company, so much of your work will be about distilling a path forward to a more inclusive and diverse team with maximized impact locally and strong communication and change management along the way. Illustratively, the work will include:

- Partner with senior leadership, HR, and Employee Resource Groups
- Cross-functional engagement and collaboration at all levels of our organization to align on and successfully manage change (in the Diversity and Belonging space, social impact, and via high-quality communication channels)
- Lead our volunteer team to new heights of community service and impact
- Ensure company communication channels, both internal and external (in partnership with Marketing) are effective and meaningful

How You'll Be Measured

Our goals are big and we're not talking "check the box" here. Some of the ways we'll measure success include:

- Effectiveness and trustworthiness of systemic changes designed to increase diversity and sense of belonging across the organization
- Attraction and retention of diverse top talent
- Improved and innovative communication and change management strategies
- Increased brand awareness for us as a brand intent on positive social change
- Engagement, satisfaction, and participation levels of our volunteer, communications, and ERGs
- Successful benefits corporation certification in the future

What We're Looking For

This role represents an incredible opportunity to empower our team and business to embrace diversity and have an even greater positive impact on the world around us. With that, we've set our sights high:

- Significant experience in Diversity, Equity, and Inclusion–centric work
- Track record of success as a people leader
- Proven leadership capabilities: leading and inspiring large groups, developing and nurturing team members
- Experience in true systemic change management related to diversity and inclusion
- Exceptional communication and presence; have been the face of similar programs internally and externally
- Proven ability to align function focused efforts with larger organization goals and objectives
- Stellar project and change management capabilities
- Strong and tested ability to build relationships and network, especially when sensitive, uncomfortable topics are the focus
- Exceptional emotional intelligence
- Great business acumen and critical thinking skills
- Comfort with traveling up to ~25% of the time to ensure support for our teams locally (of course, this may be down the road as we continue to navigate the pandemic)

In addition, you must share our company values.

Chief Diversity Officer

Our growth story is only beginning and we're looking for a Chief Diversity Officer who will champion, promote, and drive our diversity and inclusion initiatives working across all of our functions globally. Leveraging your past learnings and business-orientated approach, you'll build on our strong foundation, developing a diversity and inclusion framework that connects our mission and business strategy for growth. You'll scale our diversity and inclusion efforts, fostering a work environment where all voices are heard and validated, instilling a deep sense of belonging within our unique culture.

As a member of the Executive Team, reporting to the CEO, the CDO will partner with other members of the Executive Team and functional leaders, with especially close collaboration with the CHRO. You'll bring all of the elements of who you are into your work and invite others to do the same, creating an environment of awareness, acceptance, and allyship throughout our global organization. This role is pivotal to our company, our culture, and the authentic experience of each of our employees on a daily basis.

What You'll Do and Achieve

- Expand our initial strategic roadmap for diversity and inclusion into a robust plan that aligns our diversity and inclusion goals with our business outcomes based upon our current state and business strategy.

- Further integrate a sense of diversity and inclusion through innovative programs and initiatives that build awareness, allyship, and capabilities across the company and enhance both the employee and candidate experience.

- Provide subject matter expertise, coaching, and education with our executive and senior leadership team to inform their personal leadership and organizational strategy to advance functional and key business outcomes.

- Work closely with the Talent Acquisition team, senior leaders, and hiring managers to help build effective sourcing and selection processes, as well as progressive ways to hire, develop, promote, and retain a diverse workforce.

- Provide leadership and support to evolve the Employee Resource Group (ERG) strategy to empower and strengthen our internal communities, ensuring their impact and effectiveness across the organization and culture.

- Identify KPIs and develop an approach to assess progress, achievement, and accountability within the company and partner with the HR team to measure the impact and effectiveness of diversity and inclusion initiatives and the overall impact on culture and the employee experience.

- Strategically align with outside organizations to help augment our strategy and push beyond "best practice" to innovate and create ground-breaking thought-leadership.

- Serve as a thought leader, leveraging your strong voice to evangelize diversity and inclusion at our company and in the broader industry.

- Work in coordination with our philanthropic efforts to amplify D&I within the organization through strategic partnerships and employee engagement efforts.

What You'll Need to Be Successful

- 10+ years professional experience, including experience leading the diversity, equity, inclusion, and belonging space at high-growth companies.

- Thrive in a fast-paced driven culture with a call to get shift done.

- Proven track record of developing diversity and inclusion frameworks that connect to an organization's mission and business strategy for growth and scalability.

- Deep understanding and strong application of the concepts related to diversity and inclusion, as well as organizational structures that impact the implementation and management of effective change efforts.

- Experience activating global teams and cross-functional partners to operationalize successful diversity and inclusion programs at scale with impact within and outside of North America.

- Strong project/program management skills with a demonstrated effectiveness in the following: data analysis, interpersonal communication, consulting, facilitation, influencing, and people leadership.

- Ability to take calculated risks, push your learning edge, show up as a leader (even when doing so is hard), and motivate others to do the same.

Head of Belonging

Position Summary

The Head of Belonging will drive value across all functions and geographies by defining and reinforcing an enterprise-wide Diversity, Inclusion, and Belonging strategy that ensures as a global organization we continue to fulfill and exceed our commitments to building and nurturing an organization that encourages and values diverse perspectives in our workplace, which ultimately allows us to deliver for our patients living with rare and devastating diseases. This strategy will foster a sense of connection and community, so employees and patients know their uniqueness is not just tolerated but embraced, and that at our company, no matter who you are, you belong. We are seeking an individual who has deep knowledge around what it takes to deliver and integrate a Diversity, Inclusion, and Belonging Strategy tied to business performance. We are a fast-paced and dynamic environment; this role requires a pragmatic individual who can deliver solutions that meet immediate business needs, yet also plan for programs that align with the future vision for the company.

This individual will partner with colleagues in the broader Human Experience function, employees, business leaders, and consulting partners/vendors to analyze, design, test, and implement.

This individual will report directly to the Senior Vice President of Leadership and Innovation.

Job Duties and Responsibilities

- Develop and implement a sustainable enterprise-wide Diversity, Inclusion, and Belonging vison and strategy that enfolds both employees and patients.

- Build relationships with key leaders to create awareness, support, and advocacy for diversity and inclusion effort, reaching beyond the immediate programmatic scope to influence and lead change initiatives.

- Embed Diversity, Inclusion, and Belonging perspectives and practices so that leaders/business functions have ownership and investment in the work, and that diversity and inclusion efforts are not the exclusive area of the Human Experience Function. Design and deliver training related to workplace inclusion and unconscious bias.

- Manage multiple global/cross functional and concurrent program related projects that range in size and complexity. Using global perspectives and research D&I trends.

- Coach the Executive Committee to keep the principles of the Diversity, Inclusion, and Belonging Strategy at the forefront of their minds by constantly challenging them to authentically see and hear every employee and patient they interact with, ensuring leaders under them do the same.

- Create an environment where employees and patients can thrive, have their voices heard, and live up to their potential by infusing Diversity, Inclusion, and Belonging in our enterprise-wide programs.

- Ensure there are systems in place to measure our progress on our Diversity, Inclusion, and Belonging journey.

- Represent Diversity, Inclusion, and Belonging externally (e.g., to media, industry, and community events, networks, and conferences), communicating our commitment widely and bringing best practices and latest thinking back into the organization.

- Navigate uncharted territory where no process or precedent exists, whilst maintaining compliance with current internal procedures and industry regulations/guidance documents.

Essential Qualifications

- Proven track record of facilitating enterprise-level initiatives with multiple senior stakeholders

- Ability to build strong networks within the organization and influence change

- High tolerance for ambiguity and ability to create clarity for others; high level of organizational maturity and ability to apply judgment

- Strategy design, program development, and management experience

- Excellent oral and written communication skills, including the ability to organize and present information in a clear and concise way

- Comprehensive knowledge of D&I concepts and KPI measurements

- Current knowledge of best practices in promoting an inclusive workplace, including effective approaches to recruitment and retention

- Experienced change leader; equally comfortable in the boardroom and facilitating employee discussions

- Has experience with Citizenship/Corporate Social Responsibility and Sustainability vision and mission to ensure alignment and aim for even more future-focused efforts in those arenas

Preferred Qualifications

- Bachelor's degree; master's degree preferred

Looking at Accountability

As I review these and many other job descriptions, what always stands out to me is the expectation that the successful candidate will, as one company describes, "successfully manage change (in the Diversity and Belonging space, social impact, and via high-quality communication channels)" or from another, "Navigate uncharted territory where no process or precedent exists, whilst maintaining compliance with current internal procedures and industry regulations/guidance documents." I'm not suggesting these things can't be accomplished and as descriptions go, these aren't asking for the *whole* world. But where the disconnect lies is in the level of accountability and authority these individuals would need to have to accomplish these gargantuan tasks.

What do I suggest? My recommendation is to stop hiring Chief Diversity Officers or VPs of inclusion and diversity when you don't intend to allow them to do the work they have been hired to do. In many instances, these job descriptions are a smoke screen. They're a signal to the world that the company has a plan and intends to take some action. And while they're safely off the radar of the cancel culture, they can stall and put up barriers to progress by saying, "Our board of directors won't agree to this change," or "We don't do things this way," or my favorite, "We don't have the resources allocated for that."

What an Effective CDO Does

In your mind, you believe that you want your Chief Diversity Officer to do the work, but if you take an objective view of the role, you know that to be effective, a CDO would need to:

- Report directly to the CEO
- Have dotted-line oversight of the heads of each division within your company
- Have a direct report in each division of the company whose responsibility is to ensure that division is implementing the programs recommended by the CDO
- Have the authority to make recommended personnel changes, regardless of the seniority of the person
- Hold individuals accountable to the values and the strategy that is set by the senior leaders of the company

Be an Authentic Leader

One job description includes the request for the CDO to "Coach the Executive Committee to keep the principles of the Diversity, Inclusion, and Belonging Strategy at the forefront of their minds by constantly challenging them to authentically see and hear every employee and patient they interact with, ensuring leaders under them do the same." This is essentially what a CDO should be doing. However, remember Charles Scharf, Wells Fargo CEO (see Chapter 5)? He subsequently posted a statement, not an apology, as most leaders do once they've been caught with their foot in their mouth saying something in public that they think in private. His statement, posted on the Wells Fargo social media accounts, was "I am sorry my comment has been misinterpreted. The financial industry and our company do not reflect the diversity of our population. We, at Wells Fargo, are committed to driving change and improving diversity and inclusion."

Do you sense sincerity in that statement? Does authenticity jump out at you? The problem with bad publicity is that sneaky little bias called the bandwagon effect (see Chapter 2). Everyone likes to jump on the bandwagon and buy what everyone else is buying or wear what everyone else is wearing. However, when it comes to the negative effects, it works just the same. People started digging. They wanted to know – if Charles Scharf feels this way, what does the rest of his senior leader team think? What has their Chief Diversity Officer done? There is indeed a Chief Diversity Officer of Wells Fargo and she is unsurprisingly a Black woman who, from her LinkedIn profile, has had very little to say about diversity and inclusion during her tenure. Questions that are now being asked are "Did she prep him for the meeting with Black employees and provide him with talking points and metrics? If she did in fact do that, was she ignored? Is she a victim of his bias, or his accomplice?"

Senior diversity leaders cannot serve two masters. They are asked to create programs to protect and benefit the employees of the organization while working for the organization that is responsible for hurting those individuals. And in many cases, they are also being tasked with shielding senior leaders from negative feedback that may damage their egos. It's the same problem HR is attempting to battle while they resolve sexual harassment and other complaints and it's why in most instances, to be successful, those complaints have to go to an outside agency in order to be handled appropriately.

Creating a Role for Success

The person in this role needs to be able to speak freely and that is difficult to do when you are an employee. It's impossible to do in a team of one. Think about corporate mergers and acquisitions – there are whole teams set up to make those changes happen. They spend months preparing for the transaction, evaluating employees, reviewing job descriptions, and analyzing which employees are contributing to the new strategy and which ones will probably need to be fired. They obtain data on what the effects might be, impact to revenue, how to retain high performers, and how productivity might suffer. If I haven't been clear, a Chief Diversity Officer cannot do this work alone.

So whose job is it to embed diversity and inclusion into your company? I've already demonstrated that it isn't the job of the Chief Diversity Officer alone. It isn't the job of the few Black, LGBTQ, or female employees. And it isn't the job of the various Employee Resource Groups (ERGs). It also isn't the job of HR. But if it were the job of HR, they should have an easier path to success because they already have an entire department, they already have teams of individuals who are focused on the business, but what they don't have is the requisite authority and they have not been tasked appropriately with driving this strategy – at least not yet. But sticking with an HR model, I suggest a hybrid model where the CDO heads a department that manages staff housed in each function of the company. Those staff members can then be specialists who help craft policies that can be adapted as needed but maintain consistency across the organization by liaising with each other to maintain effective communication and avoid duplications and inefficiencies.

I believe this model would also help Chief Diversity Officers be more empowered and effective in their roles. Diversity specialists within each function of the company allow for more flow-down of information to teams as well as cross-functional and interdepartmental communication of challenges that arise. Those diversity specialists directly report to the Chief Diversity

Officer (CDO), who then reports to the company's CEO. This model allows for a more thorough integration of diversity and inclusion and places the responsibility of compliance on all of the leaders, rather than only the CDO.

Moving Past the Naysayers

An additional question you may ask is how should we or do we move forward without leaving anyone behind or alienating large populations of the workforce and/or customer base? If you look back to the discussion on equity where I explained the difference between equality and equity, you'll remember the depiction of the individuals in front of a wall (see Chapter 8). Figure 13.1 shows that there is no wall. The barrier has been removed. That is your job: to identify the barriers and then to remove them. Remember that and keep your eye on the prize.

People don't like change, but what they really have an issue with is fear of the unknown. They aren't sure what's on the other side of change and if you haven't given them a good idea of what the new outcome will look like, people will resist. A change in

FIGURE 13.1   Remove Barriers.

status is another reason people don't appreciate change. If a potential change is perceived as affecting job security, access to power, or access to information, these potential negative outcomes will also create resistance. And frontline employees like change far less than company leaders do because frontline leaders have to execute the change, and most of the time they haven't been consulted on what that change should be. In your quest to drive change, employee input should be gathered, it should be considered, and where that input was put into action should be communicated. Regardless, you will find outliers. Not everyone will agree with the change(s). Not everyone will want to change, but what you'll find, and what I've observed from the surveys we've conducted across many companies, is that the largest portion of your workforce will be fence-sitters. They will be unsure of your intentions, they will be unsure of the expected outcome, and they will take on a wait-and-see attitude.

The answer to the question of how to move forward with diversity and inclusion strategies without alienating some of the people is to let them leave, if that is what they choose to do.

Your promoters are key to change. Identify the individuals who will support your attempts to make change. Harness the energy of those who think you should have made policy changes years ago. Give the tools and resources to the people who want to help drive the bus because the fence-sitters will come along for the ride. Create opportunities for those who are unsure to learn more by spending time with your promoters. Positive attitudes are contagious, but so are negative ones. It is critical to understand that the detractors, the ones who are dead set against change, will undermine your efforts if you give them the opportunity. Don't let them. Instead, focus your energy on the promoters who will nudge the individuals in the middle and eventually the detractors will make room for more promoters. It isn't your job to attempt to appease detractors, because they will only continue to resist. The more time and attention you put into this, the more time and attention you'll have to spend with no positive result for either of you.

Leaders have to make the decisions that need to be made for the greater good based on sound information and good council. If your earnest desire is for your company to be a place where diversity is sought after, valued, and included, you may need to do a bit of pruning to make space for those who share your values. Employee resource groups, leadership, managers, frontline employees, vendors, and even your clients – they can all help drive change. But the bottom line is that it is the job of the senior leaders to define the values, create the strategy, authorize the necessary change, create accountability, and maintain progress. It is your job to lead and we expect you to rise to the occasion.

Sustaining Change

Company leaders spend a lot of time asking about best practices. They want to know how they're doing as they relate to their competitors to ensure they're not getting left behind, but when you're constantly looking in the rearview mirror to see what others behind you are doing, that doesn't help you create forward-looking policies. Benchmarking against best practices is not what you should be striving for. Instead, creating an evolutionary practice is how you drive change.

Looking to the future requires your attention to be solving for the direction you want to go, not looking at where you have been. This leads to asking your leadership team what practices, policies, or procedures are you investing time in today that won't matter in ten years? Should your company really be devoting this much time to where people work instead of how they work? Spending time dictating what degree they have instead of what capacity they have for learning or what experience they can bring to the table?

Corporate dress codes have changed drastically over the last 50 years, but we don't even have to go that far back to remember just how much they've changed. In 1999, I was working for a large law firm in New York City and dress codes were a thing. A pretty big thing. You could not come to work in anything other than a suit. And then casual Friday got implemented and many trees were killed in the writing, printing, and distributing of the updated dress code. Many hours were spent ensuring adherence to the new dress code. Many dollars were lost as employees were sent home without pay for violating said dress code. It seems like overkill now considering the extent to which that dress code was scrutinized – the billable hours spent by attorneys determining whether it was legal or prudent to move forward and inform employees that they could not, under any circumstances, wear acid-wash jeans, ripped jeans, sneakers, flip flops, low-cut blouses, shorts, or open-toed shoes to the office.

The next feature box displays the executive summary of a survey that was conducted by a State Farm Office on November 17, 2000. Pages and pages were written analyzing the survey results to determine whether to remain business casual and what that might do for their employees as well as their clients. There was definite validity to the question at the time and I'm not suggesting you ignore current-day sentiment that will need to be addressed, but there are greater priorities at hand. We only need to rewind to less than two decades ago, when CEOs began briefing their stakeholders wearing jeans and Nirvana T-shirts, to see that dress standards have evolved as a product of their environment.

Executive Summary

State Farm Insurance Company has committed itself to delivering the highest-quality customer service each and every time. The current dress policy plays a major role in achieving the company's goal. Therefore, State Farm's "business casual" dress policy should remain unchanged.

A survey of 50 individuals (25 policyholders/25 employees) was conducted at the Rock Hill Claims Office to discover their opinions on this issue. Seventy-two percent of policyholders and ninety-two percent of employees responded as being in favor of State Farm's current dress policy. This report discusses the benefits of "business casual" dress policies.

Remaining "business casual" would be very advantageous. The current dress policy allows business to be more personal. It helps to put clients at ease and speak openly about their situations. Employees would also continue to benefit from business casual dress, because it helps create a more relaxed work environment. The attire is comfortable, and it saves money on wardrobe expenses. The current dress policy is a plus for State Farm.

In the same way, it's important that we, as well as whatever practices or initiatives we set out to implement in our workplace, are flexible enough to continually adjust to changing environments. It seems laughable to think that only 50 years ago women were prohibited from wearing pants to work. It begs the question, though – what policies or procedures are we holding on to that our grandchildren will be scoffing at in only a few decades?

With the emerging issues that have breached the surface in 2020, hiring a diversity and inclusion strategist has emerged as a best practice for companies across the board. For others, it is unconscious bias education or the formation of a DEI council. You have to ask yourself, is this part of a process to flip the company's culture inside out and get to the bottom of the conscious and unconscious biases, or is this a way to "check the box" for your consumers and other stakeholders? Which is the *best* practice for your company? Are you seeking optics to pacify, or implement an effort toward real and continuous change?

Your employees will help you make the determination of where your priorities lie if you listen to the data as you seek to answer: "What conditions have we created that maintain barriers to entry or advancement for certain groups and what are we doing to remedy them?"

Resources

Industry Associations/Professional Organizations

Accounting/Finance

Accounting and Financial Women's Alliance, www.afwa.org

American Institute of Certified Public Accountants, www.aicpa.org

American Institute of Professional Bookkeepers, www.aipb.org

Association of Chartered Certified Accountants, www.accaglobal.com

Association of Credit and Collection Professionals, www.acainternational.org

Chartered Institute of Management Accountants, www.cimaglobal.com

Institute of Management Accountants, www.imanet.org

International Federation of Accountants, www.ifac.org

National Association of Black Accountants, www.nabainc.org

National Association of Insurance and Financial Advisors, www.naifa.org

National Association of Tax Professionals, www.natptax.com

Advertising/Marketing

Advertising Specialty Institute, www.asicentral.com
American Academy of Advertising, www.aaasite.org
American Marketing Association, https://www.ama.org/
Association of National Advertisers, www.ana.net
Promotional Products Association International, www.ppai.org

Business/General

Association of Latino Professionals for America, www.alpfa.org
Hispanic Alliance for Career Enhancement, https://www.haceonline.org
National Alliance on Mental Illness, www.nami.org
National Association of African Americans in Human Resources, www.naaahr.org
National Association of Negro Business and Professional Women's Clubs, http://nanbpwc.org
National Association of Women Business Owners, www.nawbo.org
National Black MBA Association, www.nbmbaa.org
Prospanica, www.prospanica.org
Step Up Women's Network, www.suwn.org

Engineering

American Indian Science and Engineering Society, https://www.aises.org
American Society of Civil Engineers, www.asce.org
Great Minds in STEM, http://www.greatmindsinstem.org
Institute of Industrial and Systems Engineers, www.iienet.org
International Society of Certified Electronics Technicians, https://www.iise.org

MAES, Latinos in Science and Engineering, http://mymaes.org

National Society of Black Engineers, www.nsbe.org

National Society of Professional Engineers, www.nspe.org

Out in Science, Technology, Engineering, and Mathematics, www.ostem.org

Society for Advancement of Hispanics/Chicanos and Native Americans in Science, https://www.sacnas.org

Society of Hispanic Professional Engineers, https://www.shpe.org

Society of Women Engineers, www.swe.org

Sales

National Association of Women Sales Professionals, www.nawsp.org

National Organization for Diversity in Sales and Marketing, https://www.minoritymarketshare.com

National Sales Network, www.salesnetwork.org

Sales Management Association, www.salesmanagement.org

Strategic Account Management Association, www.strategicaccounts.org

Technology

Afrotech, www.afrotech.com

American Association of Blacks in Energy, https://www.aabe.org

Association for Information Systems, www.aisnet.org

Black Data Processing Associates, www.bdpa.org

Cloud Computing Association, www.cloudcomputingassn.org

CompTIA, https://www.comptia.org

Hispanic IT Executive Council, https://hitecglobal.org

IEEE Communications Society, www.comsoc.org

Latinos in Information Sciences and Technology Association, https://techlatino.org

National Organization of Gay and Lesbian Scientists and Technical Professionals, www.noglstp.org

Rails Girls, www.railsgirls.com

Ruby Central, www.rubycentral.org

Society for Information Management, www.simnet.org

Software & Information Industry Association, www.siia.net

Tech America, www.techamerica.org

Women in Technology

AnitaB.org, https://anitab.org

Black Girls Code, http://www.blackgirlscode.com

DC Web Women, https://dcwebwomen.org

Girl Develop It, https://www.girldevelopit.com

Girls in Tech, https://girlsintech.org

Girls Who Code, https://girlswhocode.com

National Center for Women & Information Technology, https://www.ncwit.org

Women in Technology International, https://witi.com

Women Who Tech,- https://www.womenwhotech.com

Women 2.0, https://women2.com

LINKEDIN GROUPS

African American Women in Science, Technology, Engineering & Math, https://www.linkedin.com/groups/4412887

Black Women in Science and Engineering, https://www.linkedin.com/groups/8428298/

Blacks in Technology, https://www.linkedin.com/groups/1415387

Women in Science, Engineering & Technology, https://www.linkedin.com/groups/2417876

Women in Technology Sales, https://www.linkedin.com/groups/6993922

Women Who Tech, https://www.linkedin.com/groups/87431

Tech Savvy Women (TSW), https://www.linkedin.com/groups/124180

About the Author

Stacey A. Gordon is the Chief Diversity Strategist of Rework Work, where she focuses on reworking how companies work, including how they inclusively recruit, hire, and engage employees, effectively creating inclusion and belonging for all. She earned her MBA from the Pepperdine University School of Business and now teaches classes in Inclusive Leadership and Workplace Culture as an adjunct professor at her alma mater.

Stacey is the creator of the popular Unconscious Bias course on LinkedIn Learning, which has been translated into four languages, as well as the number one course on writing a resume. In total, her courses have accumulated more than one million views. As a consultant and career strategist, Stacey has written career- and diversity-related articles and provided content for Society for Resource Management (SHRM), *Fast Company*, Skillsoft, Forbes, NPR, BBC Radio, *Essence* magazine, and Monster.com, to name a few. She was also a career segment guest contributor to Fox Business and is a frequently requested keynote speaker around the globe.

Passionate about improving reworking work for both employers and employees, Stacey has been recognized by Pepperdine University as a Top 40 Over 40 Leader and by *Forbes* as a Top 3 Business Leader Who Spoke Out About Diversity & Inclusion. She has also earned both her Inclusive Workplace Culture credential and her SHRM Senior Certified Professional certification.

Acknowledgments

Special thanks to my family, who have supported me along the way. From my parents to my husband, to my sister and my three daughters, they have allowed me the space and time needed to write this book. I would also like to thank my work family at Rework Work who have helped me grow and sustain my ability to work with companies around the globe in the creation of strategies to improve and enhance diversity, inclusion, equity, and belonging at work. Finally, I'd also like to thank my crew of DEI consultants and friends who are always there to lend an ear, a resource, a laugh, or a meal.

Index